To Connie &

May this story be a
voice for the voiceless.

God Bless You

_Ka___ J. Zol___

9-11-18

The Will To Survive

By Karen Zale

THE WILL TO SURVIVE

"Out of suffering have emerged the strongest souls; the most massive characters are seared with scars." -- **Khalil Gibran**

Introduction

This is a true story about a World War II soldier who, against all odds, survived the Bataan Death March, the Hell Ships, and three and one-half years as a prisoner of war under the Japanese. The dehumanization and being reduced to live as an animal, amidst the continual abuse and cruelty suffered, cannot be adequately articulated.

Despite these horrors he found light at the end of the tunnel and took control of the demons that would not let go of their tenacious grip.

John would say, "How would I begin to tell my story? Where would I start? And if I told it, nobody would believe it anyway." How does a former prisoner of war who suffered unimaginable torture, pain, and agony try to have others understand what he endured? As the daughter of a World War II ex-prisoner of war, it is incumbent upon me to tell the story of human sacrifice and valor in the face of their Japanese captors (an enemy they had little if any knowledge of), which would change their lives and ours forever. An indelible mark had been made on the lives of the young men who enlisted to fight for democracy and freedom when their country called.

Every story has to start somewhere. So, here I sit in the solitude and peace of the woods left to me by my father, with trees towering overhead and the musty scent of the ground after I shuffled through the dead leaves that piled up over the years. Nearby, I observe a flock of wild turkey, two hens and eleven babies, unaware of my presence. For Dad, this was a haven -- a place to escape from tormented thoughts of years past. This is where I will start to tell his story, one that he was unable or unwilling to share until much later in life.

The irony of capturing this moment of tranquility and quietness is that, just moments ago, I was target shooting into a root ball of a fallen tree. Target in place at 30 feet, ear and eye protection on, concentrating on sight alignment and trigger control, then bam, bam, bam, bam, bam, bam.....six out of six in the bulls-eye. The first practice round was with a Smith and Wesson .357 magnum handgun, followed by "The Judge," using .45 caliber Colt rounds. The 9mm Belgium Nazi war souvenir was left at home. Dad made sure his daughter learned at an early age how to handle a handgun. Little did I know at that young age why he was teaching me certain skills. The contrast was quite startling between loud gunfire and spent shells and the solitude of the woods. Just as Dad's thoughts wavered between being in the thick of combat and his finding solace on his acreage in the country, even more irony came from making the decision to start telling his story while enjoying the outdoors with no paper on which to write. So, I turned over the targets and started to write these words.

After locking the handguns and ammo in the trunk of my car, a peaceful hike on these beautiful 101 acres of woodland ensued. Oh, look, there's a "Mayapple" already gone past her time of ripe fruit. Back when my brother,

Allen, and I were just young kids, Dad was always pointing out "survival" food. He would show us the "Jewel Weed" and explain how you can rub the juice from the plant on your skin if you get into poison ivy. The round galls on the stems of "Golden Rod" contained edible worms. His lessons were subtle and he secretly had good reason to instruct his two children on how to "survive."

Today, it is roughly fifty years later after Dad's impromptu, yet deliberate, lessons. It is hot and muggy here in the Southern Tier of New York State and the flies are a nuisance. It is uncomfortable to stay in one spot too long, otherwise the flies form this little swarm around your head and an occasional deer fly zaps your scalp. Dad knew about flies from his prisoner of war days; flies were an additional enemy they had to fight in the tropical heat of the Philippine Islands. But this country property was Dad's sanctuary. It was a place where he could control his life and his destiny. No one could harm him here. The Japanese would not enter into his world here.

Chapter 1

The Early Years

John Zubrzycki, who in 1950 changed his name to John Zale, seemed to be predestined to endure the path that was yet to unfold before him. A rough childhood became his training ground. His fortitude sprouted from his Polish heritage.

Wind back the hands of time back to an era that was pre-World War I, when the United States had a great influx of immigrants. There was a wave of those from Eastern Europe who sought refuge in America around 1890, including many from Poland.

Over a long period of history, Poland fought against Russia, Ukraine, Austria, and Germany which lead to the partitioning of the country among various factions several times. As the result of centuries of warfare, the Poles were reduced to serfs working on rich farmlands claimed and owned by the nobility.

Life was hard – a daily struggle with a dim future. Stories were told of my great grandmother, Eufrosine Zdyb, working the farm of such a landowner. Wearing her babushka (a traditional head scarf), her skin was ruddy and weather beaten. Interrupting her work one day, she gave birth to her baby and went right back into the fields to continue her back-breaking labor. The place they called home was just a hovel with dirt floors.

Poles were emigrating to escape their abject poverty. They heard stories of America, where the streets were paved with gold and opportunity beckoned. Poverty, warfare, and turbulent times were strong motivators for those who dreamed of a better life.

Shortly before World War I, between 1909 and 1913, our family's ancestors set sail from Poland to seek a new and better life in America. They included my paternal grandparents, Piotr (Peter) Paul Zubrzycki, and Zofia (Sophie) Zdyb. Also among those to pass through Liberty and Ellis Islands were my maternal grandparents, Stanislaw (Stanley) Antonik and Janina (Jennie) Karpinska.

Approaching Liberty Island in New York Harbor, these weary travelers must have been awestruck at the sight of the Statue of Liberty; her arm raised to the sky holding the torch as their ship inched closer to shore. Lady Liberty had these words of welcome: "Give me your tired, your poor, your huddled masses yearning to breathe free. The wretched refuse of your teeming shore. Send these, the homeless, tempest-tossed, to me: I lift my lamp beside the golden door."[1]

These four dreamers made the long voyage across the Atlantic Ocean. What brave souls, to leave behind the only life they knew and courageously sail to an unknown land where they didn't even speak the language. Their destination was Lackawanna, a city south of Buffalo, New York. They soon discovered the streets were not paved with gold, but were covered with soot that belched from the furnaces of the Bethlehem Steel Company, where many immigrants found employment at "the Plant."

Ultimately, Stanislaw Antonik and Janina Karpinska wed and lived on Sand Street in Lackawanna. They had eight children: My mother Stella, born in 1926, was the number four child; her siblings were Stanley, Jr., Henry, Joseph, Norbert, Matthew, Phyllis, and Anthony. The

---

[1] Quote by Emma Lazarus

family was a little better off, compared to the living conditions of other Poles "on the other side of the tracks." Another reference given to that same area was "the other side of the bridge." Stella had been lectured that girls did not date boys from "the other side" and they were to be avoided.

Piotr Zubrzycki and Zofia Zdyb were among the unfortunate families who *did* settle on the other side of the tracks on Wasson Avenue after they wed. They had three children, all born in the house: My father, John, born in 1922, and then his sister, Frances, and his brother, Marion (nicknamed Shorty). Others were discouraged to mingle with the rough and tumble folks on this side of the bridge, who were the poorest of the poor. When John was five years old, the family moved to Ingham Avenue, a block away from the railroad tracks.

The Zubrzycki family from left to right: Frances, Piotr, Marion, Zofia, John

Piotr was uneducated and illiterate. Only Polish was spoken at home and the children became bi-lingual. Zofia was motivated to become a United States citizen and studied diligently while raising the children and running a small candy store in the front portion of their living quarters on Ingham Avenue. The tragic part is that Piotr would spend a large portion of his earnings at the local watering holes, which left little money for buying food. He would find his way after work at the plant to the gin mill for a short snort. A shot-in-the-beer lead to two, then three -- or more. Piotr had a bad temper and, fueled by booze, he would not hesitate to give the family a beating when he got home. Back in those days, neighbors looked the other way in matters of domestic violence.

The Zubrzyckis lived in poverty and hunger pangs were a way of life. Johnny was berated by a hotdog-stand owner when the hungry boy poured gobs of ketchup on a small hotdog. This was one way to get some extra food into his growling stomach. Zofia would cook some of the traditional Polish dishes she learned as a girl: *czernina* (duck blood soup), *galareta* (pigs feet in an aspic-like gelatin) topped with vinegar, and *sledź with cebulą* (raw herrings with onion). Perhaps taste buds are less discerning when one is very hungry! The family raised rabbits in the backyard for food. Piotr showed Johnny only one time how to kill and skin the rabbits. After that, it became Johnny's responsibility to be in charge of taking care of the rabbits and providing them as food for the table.

Winters were bitterly cold in Lackawanna with strong winds blowing in from Lake Erie. The Zubrzyckis house would feel like a refrigerator during those long, cold months. Water in the toilet would freeze--it was one of those old-fashioned toilets where the water was in a tank overhead and a pull-chain would cause the water to flush downwards.

The indoor plumbing did not include hot water. Any time hot water was needed, it was heated on top of the stove. Bath time (as infrequent as it was) proved to be a challenge, since the water had to be heated first. Bathing was nothing more than a simple act of utilizing a small tub with the now-heated water placed in the sink.

The pot-bellied stove served as a furnace. It burned coal, but coal was expensive and in short supply at this house. Johnny and his brother would go down to the nearby railroad tracks to scrounge up coal. The boys would climb on top of the open gondola cars and kick the coal down to the ground where it was quickly gathered and taken home before the local police could catch them.

Once the evening coals burned out, no fire would be made again until the morning and heat rapidly escaped through the home's thin walls. Frost formed on the walls inside of their bedroom and the boys would scrape it with their fingernails. Zofia would heat a brick and wrap it in a towel for the children to take to bed to provide some warmth. The life saver was the big goose-down blanket, a feather bed called a *pierzyna*, that Johnny and Shorty shared as they slept in the same bed. The boys would dive under the *pierzyna,* which provided a toasty warm sanctuary against the frozen air.

The era known as Prohibition started in 1920 with the ratification of the 18th Amendment to the U.S. Constitution, which banned the making, selling, or transporting of alcoholic beverages. The Amendment was finally replaced in 1933 with the ratification of the 21st Amendment. So as not to be without alcohol, Piotr set up a homemade distillery. Moonshine, as it was called, became another one of Johnny's assigned chores. The snotty-nosed little boy with his disheveled hair, wearing his knickers, would deliver the precious liquid for his father. He didn't dare stumble and break a bottle because that would result in a beating.

In 1929, when Johnny was seven years old, the Wall Street market crashed, followed by the Great Depression of 1929 to 1930. It was a world-wide economic depression and the effects lasted until the start of World War II. Those were difficult times to be growing up and Johnny became a tough boy. There was one year that he actually got a Christmas gift: An orange in a stocking.

Piotr was not a loving father and his temper was taken out on the family. Johnny would witness his mother being violently battered and, for himself along with Shorty, getting a beating was a common occurrence. Johnny would make his own beatings harder for Piotr to deliver by running in circles around his father to try to wear him out. Shorty wasn't as resourceful and would just stand there and take the punishment without putting up a fight. The only nurturing at home were the attempts made by his loving mother, who would become an inspiration to Johnny when he later became a prisoner of war (POW).

Kernels of barley had another use besides a grain to be cooked and eaten. Piotr placed the small, hard barley kernels on the floor in front of a holy picture that hung on the wall. He made Johnny kneel on the barley, facing the picture. As the kernels dug into his knees, Piotr would take his hands and press down on his son's shoulders, inflicting more pain.

Johnny did not like school. He attended Saint Hyacinth's Catholic School during grade school and his behavior would cause the nuns to hit his knuckles with a wooden ruler. Later, he attended a public elementary school where he was an unruly troublemaker. His teacher, Miss Nash, admonished Johnny, warning him that someday he would be in jail wearing a prison uniform and assigned a number. That was a very prophetic statement.

He formed a gang with his buddies from the neighborhood similar to the Dead End Kids, where survival in the streets meant loyalty to the gang. This is where loyalty became fundamental for him and would later prove to be his hallmark during the years that were fast approaching.

The boys in the gang would skip school. Being chased by the truant officer was a cat-and-mouse game they dared to play. The officer was always combing the area, trolling for these street urchins who were dodging school. Fun was had by catching crawfish at the creek and cooking them in a tin can. What an awesome, delectable treat! Shucks, this sure beat going to school and learning the Three R's: Reading, 'Riting, and 'Rithmetic.

Johnny, Shorty, and some of the boys in the neighborhood joined the Polish Boy Scouts, which was part of the Polish National Alliance. They learned how to march, performed calisthenics, and learned Polish traditions. Johnny was allured by the structure, camaraderie, and discipline of the scouts, which gave him a taste of belonging to something bigger than his bleak world. He felt as though he wanted to be a leader and not just of his neighborhood gang. He had an innate sense of responsibility and was driven to help others.

Polish Boy Scouts; arrow indicates John

There was one hot, summer day at the local swimming hole when Shorty started to drown. Johnny didn't think twice about jumping into the water and saving his little brother's life. They didn't dare tell their father about this event. It was similar to the time when Johnny stepped on an iron spike, as they often went barefoot to not wear out their shoes. They pulled out the spike and their dog licked the wound. This was a far better alternative to having their father finding out, knowing all too well that the outcome would be an unsympathetic beating.

Johnny quit school after the sixth grade and went to work to help the family earn a few extra dollars. Time marched on and the day came when Piotr asked his son, "How much longer do I have to keep feeding you?" Johnny knew it was time to escape this wretched life. On his 18th birthday, he asked his mother if she would be willing to sign papers so he could enlist in the Army. Later, he would say that his childhood, in the rough-and-tumble world he knew, prepared him for what was yet to come: The beatings, starvation, shivering in the cold......*survival*.

Chapter 2

Three Hots and a Cot

World War II began abroad on September 1, 1939, when John was 17 years old. The United States had not yet formally entered the war. On Valentine's Day, February 14, 1940, he and his childhood chum, Ben "Turkey" Grzybowski, headed out to the Army recruitment office. Five days earlier, John had just turned 18 and the prospect of having three square meals a day, clothes, and a place to sleep was enticing. Flicking his cigarette butt outside before entering the office, the two teenagers were soon face-to-face with the recruiter.

Sitting up straight and mustering his courage, John explains to the Army recruiter he wants to enlist immediately and be sent as far away from home as possible. Leaning forward over the desk, peering over his eyeglasses, the recruiter locks eyes with John. In a grave tone he warned this young man, "Son, that would be the Philippine Islands, but you don't want to go there. That place is sitting on a keg of dynamite and the fuse is getting shorter." John maintained he wanted to go as far away as possible and that is where he chose to serve his country.

Heading back home, he was going to inform his parents that he has joined the Army. Piotr could only be found at the local gin mill. John said, "Good-bye, Pa. I'm leaving for the Army now." Piotr was void of emotion and had nothing to say to his departing son. Nothing.

Here he was, just a teenager, who never left his hometown of Lackawanna. Now filled with adventure, off to see the world, he had 75-cents in his pocket and a one-way train ticket to New Rochelle, New York. The call is shouted, "All aboard." Klickety-klack, klickety-klack, with the rhythmic sounds of the rumbling train, what thoughts must have been swirling through his head as he embarked on this journey. The final destination was boot camp at Fort Slocum, located at the western end of Long Island Sound.

Pvt. John S. Zubrzycki of the U.S. Army's 31st Infantry Regiment, "C" Company, the "Polar Bear Regiment," also known as the American Foreign Legion. It had a special ring to it. On March 21, 1940, he writes home with all the unedited misspellings, grammar mistakes, lack of punctuation, et cetera. A three-cent postage stamp is affixed to the envelope:

"Hello Folks: --

Having a wonderful time, sorry I couldn't write sooner because we were busy going thrue the doctors and having our needles and clothes. It's pretty hard saving money because you have to take books out, "canteen books" you have to go to the barber every week even if you don't need a haircut, we had to get supplies which cost us a lot of money. We don't get paid until we leave for the Philipines that will be about April 2, 1940. They have pretty good eats 3 times a day have to take a shower, fix your own bed, wake up 6 o'clock in the morning and do some marching. We have inspection every week. Have a lot of friends go show on Saturday's free on other days you pay 20 cents. We are located on a island. We have about 73 fellows in our room. We are going to have K.P. on Sunday. We have marching drills about twice a week, we have a very strict commandor but he is O.K. We have to pay a tailor for cleaning our suits and putting holes in collars for buttons.

They have a very nice show, soft seats and ventilation.

We can walk around the islands only in particular places and no further or get put in a brig.

We have recreation halls which have basketball, poll, rest rooms with books to read, radio's to listen too and we can stay out till 11:00 P.M. o'clock but the lights go out at 9:00 P.M. There are a lot of Barracks on the island there are a couple of thousand men on it.

Sorry I can't write anymore.

Your Son
John S. Zubrzycki"

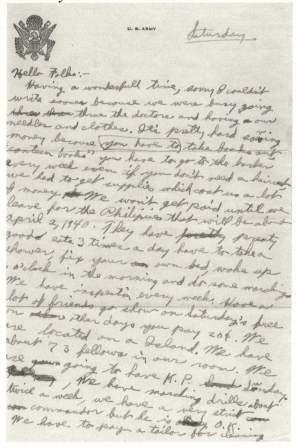

of our suits and putting holes in collars
for buttons.
They have a very nice show, soft
seats and ventilation.
We can walk around the island only
in particular places and no further
or get put in a brig.
We have recreation halls which
have, basketball, pool, rest rooms
with books to read, radio
to listen too and we can stay out till
(1:00 P.M.) o'clock but the lights go out at 9:00 P.M.
There are a lot of Barracks on the Island there
are a couple of thousand men on it.
Sorry I can't write anymore.
Your son
John J. Zubrzycki

Now earning a whopping $21 a month, the time came to ship out from New York on April 2, 1940. The route went from Charleston, South Carolina, through the Panama Canal, and ultimately departing the United States from Angel Island's Fort McDowell on the West Coast. On April 19, leaving the shore of San Francisco, California, he heard a recording of a song by Bing Crosby, "Red Sails in the Sunset."

Red sails in the sunset, way out on the sea
Oh, carry my loved one home safely to me
He sailed at the dawning, all day I've been blue
Red sails in the sunset, I'm trusting in you.

Swift wings you must borrow

Make straight for the shore
We'll marry tomorrow
And he goes sailing no more

Red sails in the sunset, way out on the sea
Oh, carry my loved one home safely to me.[2]

Sailing across the Pacific, John's blue eyes matched the sky as he scanned the vastness of the ocean. Here, he was being transported oceans away from home to a far and distant land, with hopeful prospects of experiencing the unknown.

A goal of boot camp is to transform civilians into a fighting machine. Your identity is stripped from you as you don olive drab uniforms and conform to the standards as a "GI," that is, Government Issue. John, being the cocky "street-wise" kid, apparently had not completely succumbed to this new mindset. While journeying across the Pacific, a twinkle of mischief came to his eyes. Yearning to leave his mark of individuality, he stubbornly took his pocket knife and proceeded to scratch his full name on one of the transport's brass plates.

This probably was not his smartest move, since it was readily determined who the culprit was that committed this act of vandalism! Literally caught by his own hand, he was reprimanded and spent hours scrubbing and polishing the brass until his name was removed. He learned his lesson that he was in the Army now and couldn't be the rebel from his gang days.

Then came the crossing of the International Date Line on May 9, and the soldiers aboard the transport went through an initiation called "The Ancient Order of the

---

[2] Song written by Hugh Williams, published in 1935

Deep." The initiate received a wallet-sized card stating, "This certifies that John S. Zubrzycki having crossed the INTERNATIONAL DATE LINE in the U.S.A.T. "U.S. Grant," enroute to Manila, P.I., on May 9, 1940, at 0-20 North Latitude, and having been duly initiated, then and there, into the Solemn Mysteries of the REALM OF THE RAGING MAIN, is and should be recognized and addressed as SIR SHELLBACK JOHN S. ZUBRZYCKI. By order of NEPTUNE REX, Ruler of the Raging Main and DAVY JONES, His Majesty's Scribe."

Ancient Order of the Deep

This Certifies that John S. Zubrzycki having crossed the INTERNATIONAL DATE LINE in the U.S.A.T. "U. S. GRANT," enroute to Manila, P. I., on May 9, 1940, at 0-20 North Latitude, and having been duly initiated, then and there, into the Solemn Mysteries of the REALM OF THE RAGING MAIN, is and should be recognized and addressed as:

SIR SHELLBACK John S. Zubrzycki.
                              SIGNATURE

DAVY JONES   By order of NEPTUNUS REX
His Majesty's Scribe   Ruler of the Raging Main

The trip had been utterly amazing for the wide-eyed teenager! Upon arrival, the Philippine Islands seemed like something from a postcard. What a dichotomy—such a contrast between Lackawanna and these magnificent islands. Smoggy skies, railroad tracks, and towering smoke stacks were replaced by vividly blue skies, inviting sandy beaches, and towering palm trees with their branches waving in the warm tropical breeze. Could this be the same Planet Earth?

Manila was called the "Pearl of the Orient." It was a tropical paradise with breath-taking sunsets and an atmosphere of tranquility. For the first two months, John loved everything about the Philippine Islands, but the time came to wake up from the dream and smell the coffee. The landscape didn't appear so rosy with the arrival of torrential rains from the seasonal monsoons, which added to the drudgery of day-to-day Army life.

While stationed in Manila, over the course of the next nine months, John wrote letters home. Here are some excerpts:

"June 10, 1940
Dear Folks,

Sorry that I didn't write sooner but you know how it is, the first few months are always busy.

Well I reached the Philippines safe and sound. We have rifle practice almost every day at 7:30 a.m. up to 11:00 a.m. and boy do we practice after drill we clean our rifles and oil them up. But one thing of all is that this place is pretty expensive you might not believe this but I'll show you why – laundry—1.50 and then we have to have about 8 ties, 40 shorts and 40 undershirts, 10 complete suits 40 to 50 pair of socks at least 4 pair of shoes 10 towels and about 40 hankerchiefs.

We have to pay for them ourselves and we have to have 2 to 3 pair of overhalls. You see we change our clothing at least 3 times a day. Then we have to put $5.00 to the Quarter Master for savings and at the end of our term we get it back with a 4% interest.

Then we have to pay $3.00 to the Philippine guys for doing our K.P. which I would do myself, but the majority pays so the few of us have to pay too. This might seem not true to you's but it is. I would like to know if $10.00 would be enough to send home which I know you could youse more. But I'm telling you the truth it is pretty tough over here in this heat and further more the rainy season is coming now. They say when a soldier goes out of here he is pretty good because all the places are restricted except for about 4 places. So that means that you can't go walkin around without gettin into trouble.

We are situated in a city that is surrounded by a 20 foot wall. Boy is this place crumy. They have some pigmy tribes over here in the jungle that are blood thirsty in other words wild.

Would I like to see Turkey's face right now, when he comes off the cattle boat he is going to get the surprise of his life.

The officers over here don't go for pretty good stuff you have to be perfect. What I mean is that if you shoot a rifle you can't be just pretty good, it has to be perfect and nothing else.

Haven't much more to say cause I don't know much about this place yet. By the way do you know what I saw people eat over here eggs that are half roasted in the sun, it is half chicken and half egg they call the Baulutes.

P.S. I'm doing my best to help the folks out a little as I said before this may sound like a lot of baloney to you but it is true."

"August 14, 1940
Dear Folks:

I hope the newspapers don't scare you people at home, you probably read that we have to stay an extra 18 months. A lot of trouble is brewing up but don't let that worry you, but what ever you do is don't tell Mom, o.k.

Yours forever,
Johnny
Ans. soon, if not sooner."

"December 16, 1940
Dear Folks:--

Let me tell you about my experience out on the field. We went out for a couple weeks and walked over mts. and more mts. Swam rivers with our clothing and equipment. And reaching camp at night we got beans for supper and a bean sandwich for dinner and 1 egg for breakfast slept on the hard ground with every bug in the jungle in my tent. Wake up every morning at 4:30 and get a canteen with water that's all you got all day but I made allright. We ran into snakes, lizards & other animals, and these "carobous" as you call water buffalo are pretty wild that some of them we had a little trouble with them but not much we almost had to shoot a few of them."

"March 22, 1941
Hello Folks,

Received your letter while I was out on combat problems. We were out for 2 weeks, and are moving out again for another week.

Don't forget we were shooting real bullets. We had to run afternoons, the grass was over our head and hands and as thick as a finger, so you must imagine how tough it was.

You probably won't understand what I'm talking about anyway. The afternoons were so hot that we just about breathed. After we got finished firing we had to clean our rifles wash our clothes and eat our supper. No matter how hard it gets here the better I like it.

Let me tell you about the field. We went out of our barracks to Camp O'Donell. There we camped for two weeks. We would get up in the morning about 5:30 A.M., stand revely police up around our bunks and get ready for chow. When it still was a little dark, we put on our packs and carried our rifles then we went on the range and fired on targets. We would run up the hills crawl and hide ourselves as if spying on the enemy by this time the sun got very hot, then we would get into another attack formation *and attack other targets. We had only 1 canteen of water for the morning. We would fire at airplane targets, that is a real plane pulling a sock behind it and we would fire at the sock. Then we would fire at tanks.*

Our squad consisting of 8 men were the best in our battalion so we were chosen for the Chief of Inf. Combat squad. I was the leading scout."

On May 10, 1941, John sent the following from Manila:

"RADIOGRAM: To the one and only mother. Still have not forgotten she is my best love. Your son, Johnny."

```
                    ..-RADIOGRAM
  .285   KA1HR    ck 17  Manilla   PI   May 10
                  -------------------

  To the one and only mother. Still have
  have not forgotten she is my best love.
                Your Son,
                        Johnny

          ----------------------------
  Rcvd W8PLA  May 20, and mailed by W8KYR
```

Pvt. Zubrzycki, thinking he might want to make the Army his career, studied diligently and volunteered for everything in an effort to better himself. His motivation was to move up in rank. At the end of May, 1941, he volunteered to go to an ammunition ship to get supplies to be loaded onto a barge. A typhoon hit the area with 30 to 40-foot waves. Typhoons also have the capacity to produce winds up to 140 miles-per-hour. Being tossed about on the heaving ship with battering ocean waves pouring over him, John had to tie himself down to the deck to keep from being swept overboard as he rode out the storm.

Surviving this ordeal was more excitement than he ever anticipated experiencing in the Army. In his naiveté, he thought this adventure surely was worth writing home about. On June 10, 1941, he wrote:

"Dear folks,

Received your letter dated June 4, and I sure was sorry I couldn't answer sooner. We were on guard on a ammunition boat and we stayed on it for 10 days. I just came off today and was it tough. We had a typhoon here and I toaght thet the boat would sink thats how bad it was. There was a little schooner that sunk not more than 200 yds. away from our boat But I'm glad it's over. Tomorrow we are going on a 80 mile march, it sure is going to be hard.

Don't worry about me getting killed. I'm not the least bit worried, I can use the bayonet pretty good, and that goes the same for the rifle. The soldiers don't care to read about the war in Europe so we don't care what's going on. You might know more about the war then we do, cause we don't want to know, that way we don't think about it. The conscripts have a good chance to make a rating just as good as ours, "the bunch of sisses." It's a wonder their mothers aren't there dressing them up each morning.

P.S. You sure made a lot of mistakes in the letter.
Yours forever
Johnny"

Above six photos: John Zubrzycki in the Philippine Islands prior to the bombing of Pearl Harbor

In due time, on November 3, 1941, John was promoted to corporal and put in charge of a squad of eight men. Meanwhile, back home in Lackawanna, the letters that the Zubrzyckis wrote to John and mailed to Manila on November 22nd, 23rd and December 31, 1941, were stamped, "RETURNED TO SENDER SERVICE SUSPENDED."

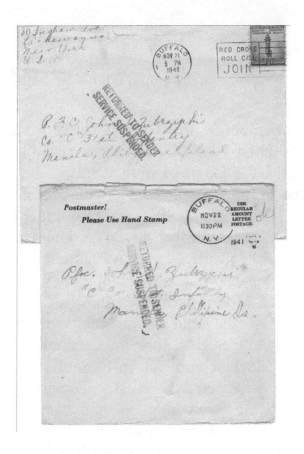

Again, just as it was throughout his childhood, his life would be "star-crossed." Upon arrival in the Islands, John was living on the edge of a dream. When the bubble burst, a long, long nightmare was just beginning.

He crossed the threshold from teenager to manhood in a matter of months. His world was turned upside down and his eyes saw terrible things beyond imagination. For the next three and one-half years, he went through Hell and back. The turning point was, "A date which will live in infamy," as bemoaned by President Franklin Delano Roosevelt.

Chapter 3

No Mama, No Papa, No Uncle Sam

On December 7, 1941, the Japanese made a sneak attack and bombed Pearl Harbor in the Hawaiian Islands. Simultaneously, the Japanese were attacking the Philippine Islands. Due to the time difference with the Islands being on the Asian side of the International Date Line, the date in the Philippines was December 8, 1941. The Army's Clark Airfield on Luzon in the Islands was utterly destroyed in short order by waves of Japanese bombers.

Now the world became embroiled in war. On December 8, 1941, the United States declared war on Japan. Nineteen-year-old Corporal Zubrzycki and the other men in his unit were caught completely off guard at the moment Clark Airfield was being bombed. Top-notch Japanese troops, who were well-supplied and supported, were landing by the droves in the Islands.

John later reflected, "The bugler blew 'Call to Arms' and no one even knew what that call meant! It took us a while to draw our weapons and ammo and get ready to move out. Everything changed at that moment and we all knew we were going for broke." They assumed they were going to fight the Japanese to the death of the last man. "All I remember is that everything was in chaos. American civilians and Filipinos got mixed in with us. The roads were jammed with vehicles and panicked people and nobody knew where they were going." The idyllic life of duty in the Islands was instantly turned upside down and inside out for the men of "C" Company, 31st Infantry Regiment.

In order to get a sense of America's enemy, consider the events that occurred abroad of just a little over two years before the start of World War II. The Japanese Imperial Army was a juggernaut of warfare. It was December, 1937, in Nanking, China, where a bloodbath of mass murder and mass rape was unleashed on the Chinese population. Over the course of six weeks, the Japanese Imperial Army brutally murdered between 200,000 and 300,000 people. Soldiers and civilians, including women and children, were executed. Not only were the women raped but the men were sodomized. Bodies littered the streets everywhere as the city was ravaged and destroyed. Soon, American and Filipino troops in the Islands would meet this monster of war in brutal combat.

The American military was deficient right from the start of their involvement in World War II. The troops were ill-equipped and had only old ammunition left over from World War I which resulted in dud rounds being fired. Soldiers of the U.S. Army's proud "Polar Bears" infantry regiment were still using old, bolt-action 1903 Springfield rifles in the new era of automatic small arms. Other weaponry and equipment was outdated as well.

Rumors abounded of miles-long supply convoys steaming across the Pacific in relief of the troops on Bataan and the island fortress of Corregidor. If they could just hang on a little longer against the Japanese invaders! However, none of the reinforcements were coming and only more rumors arrived.

The Japanese air forces were strafing and bombing the Philippine Islands at will. It was on Christmas Eve of 1941, Corporal Zubrzycki and his squad of eight men were under the command of Captain Richard K. Carnahan. They were preparing to leave Manila for the Bataan Peninsula. Rations were already meager, but John had some fruit and English walnuts. As the Japanese bombed the docked ships around him, he crushed the walnuts in his hand while frantically hitting the deck. This handful of food would be the closest thing to a real meal that he would have for the next three and one-half years.

Now on the Bataan Peninsula, the harsh reality of war hit hard. The Battle of Bataan was a momentous conflict with intense fighting as American and Filipino troops valiantly defended the peninsula. Bombs and guns that were going off everywhere made a deafening noise. Casualties were staggering. The acrid smell from the explosions burned the nostrils. The sounds of screaming men being blown apart was gut wrenching. With bodies and body parts laying everywhere, the carnage was hard to gaze upon. Many of these shell-shocked men of extraordinary devotion to duty had already made the ultimate sacrifice. In the midst of combat, emotions were running full throttle; both fear and courage mixed together. The Japanese forces were unrelenting and the bloody battle raged on and on.

With no reinforcements arriving, the men finally realized they had been abandoned and were completely on their own. The following became their mournful lament:

"No mama, no papa, no Uncle Sam
No pills, no planes, no artillery pieces
No aunts, no uncles, no nephews, no nieces
And nobody gives a damn
We are the Battling Bastards of Bataan."

There was a heavy artillery battle along the entire front, along with non-stop bombing attacks by the enemy. On January 9, 1942, the Japanese were assaulting Bataan by attacking the Philippine Army divisions that were holding the Abucay line of defense. Then, on January 16, the 51st Philippine division counterattacked in order to restore positions lost the previous day. Despite the Filipinos initially achieving success, the Japanese then pulled out all the stops and the 51st fell back in a state of panic and confusion.

Corporal Zubrzycki, as part of the US 31st Infantry in the area of the Abucay Hacienda, was ordered to counterattack. Amid the tall sugar cane, the fighting was vicious with hand-to-hand and eyeball-to-eyeball combat for the next five days. The storming Japanese were screaming the bloodcurdling sound of their battle-cry, "Banzai!"

On January 21, 1942, already having been four weeks into non-stop combat, John issued quarter rations to his squad. He divvied up one can of salmon and one can of tomatoes among eight hungry men. That day, they continued their fight in the Battle of Bataan on one of the defensive positions called the Abucay Line. The men were being pounded by a constant barrage of Japanese artillery and air force bombing. In the thick of the action, John was hit with flying shrapnel. Red hot shell fragments ripped through his stomach and up into his chest cavity. Time came to a crashing halt.

The impact of the shrapnel threw him to the ground, crumpled and numb. From the crescendo of exploding ordnance, his eardrums could only discern muffled tones, as though someone had their hands covering his ears. Dazed and looking up, all he could see were arms and legs hanging from the trees. He vomited the salmon and tomatoes eaten earlier that day. Body parts and dead soldiers covered the ground. The young infantryman thought his legs were missing. Not knowing the extent of his injuries, he believed he was on death's doorstep. Sensing life would soon be drained from him, he prayed to God to have mercy on their souls. At that moment a peace washed over him. The American troops were retreating and he was left to die.

As fate would have it, two soldiers courageously returned to survey the carnage and search for survivors. A fellow soldier from "C" Company, Sgt. Abie Abraham, along with a Filipino Scout, found Corporal Zubrzycki hanging on to life. Together, they dragged John in his blood-soaked uniform off the battlefield and carried him to a schoolhouse being used as an inadequate makeshift field hospital.

Charlie Company was in combat in the thick jungle where conditions were very primitive. This is where John was operated on. He "came to" during the surgery and saw his intestines on a table outside of his body as the shrapnel was removed. He was given a direct blood transfusion by another soldier. There was no pain medication. As he was being stitched up, his Last Rites were given. Life was in the balance. As if this weren't enough, Japanese planes were swiftly approaching the area and the patients were being frantically evacuated because the schoolhouse was going to be attacked!

John was carried out on a cot that was set down in the dirt, placed under trees, and covered with mosquito netting. Just as the men were evacuated, the building was bombed and obliterated. Sharp shards of bamboo from a nearby grove ripped through the air and impaled several defenseless patients.

While recuperating, John's company commander came to the makeshift jungle "hospital," and reported that his platoon sergeant was killed in action. Captain Carnahan said that if Zubrzycki could make it back to the unit, he would be promoted to acting platoon sergeant and would earn a third stripe. Besides his devotion to duty and his loyalty, the prospect of getting that stripe was enough motivation! John seized the opportunity and did, indeed, make it back. On March 7, 1942, he returned to service as the leader of his platoon, under regimental commander Lieutenant Colonel Jasper Brady.

In addition to leading a platoon of 64 men, the now 20-year old Sergeant Zubrzycki was also put in charge of a number of Filipino Regular Army soldiers. These men were not Filipino Scouts. John was so weak from his wounds that he was unable to carry his rifle. He assigned that chore to one of the Filipinos under his command. Shortly thereafter, John contracted malaria and was administered liquid quinine.

One of the Filipino soldiers came up to Zubrzycki with what appeared to be a "self-inflicted" wound. The Filipino's trigger finger was hanging by only a tendon. Apparently, this was a ruse to avoid be sent back into the action. Zubrzycki took his trusty pocket knife, cut the finger off the rest of the way, and ordered him to, "Get back to the line! This is *your* goddam country we're fighting for!"

In the interim, back home, the Zubrzyckis received a telegram that their son had been wounded in action.

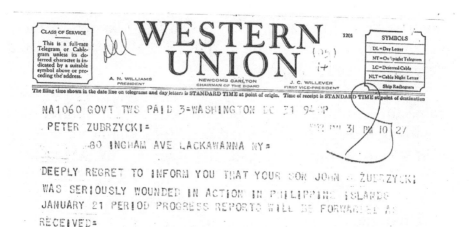

NA1060 GOVT TWS PAID 3=WASHINGTON DC 31 94 MP

PETER ZUBRZYCKI=

31 PM 10 27

80 INGHAM AVE LACKAWANNA NY=

DEEPLY REGRET TO INFORM YOU THAT YOUR SON JOHN S ZUBRZYCKI WAS SERIOUSLY WOUNDED IN ACTION IN PHILIPPINE ISLANDS JANUARY 21 PERIOD PROGRESS REPORTS WILL BE FORWARDED AS RECEIVED=

ADAMS THE ADJUTANT GENERAL.

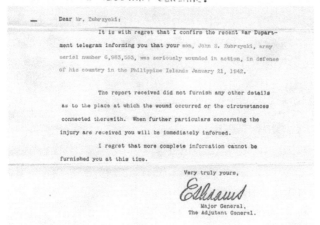

Dear Mr. Zubrzycki:

It is with regret that I confirm the recent War Department telegram informing you that your son, John S. Zubrzycki, army serial number 6,985,553, was seriously wounded in action, in defense of his country in the Philippine Islands January 21, 1942.

The report received did not furnish any other details as to the place at which the wound occurred or the circumstances connected therewith. When further particulars concerning the injury are received you will be immediately informed.

I regret that more complete information cannot be furnished you at this time.

Very truly yours,

E.F. Adams

Major General,
The Adjutant General.

Sadly, most US troops in the Philippine Islands were malnourished and starving with rations cut in half and then in quarter portions. The emaciated men were eating lizards, snakes, horse meat from the Filipino Cavalry, carabao, and monkeys. A dietary staple was a rice porridge called "lugao," which was watery rice formed to the size of a tennis ball. At times, maggots were found in the food.

While in this weakened state, the men were plagued with tropical diseases. A constant swarm of disease-carrying mosquitoes and flies infected the troops with dysentery, both wet and dry beriberi, pellagra, malaria and dengue fever. At one point early on before the battle, John contracted dengue fever and was treated with the antibiotic sulfanilamide. Quinine was in short supply. Hordes of insects infested everything and the men's mantra became, "Who die, you or the fly," as they incessantly battled this enemy as well.

The war raged on and the Battles for Bataan and Corregidor were considered the "Alamo" of World War II. "Remember Bataan" became a battle cry of revenge for American troops yet to go into combat.

For spending most of his time in his underground fortress, Overall Commanding General Douglas MacArthur was given the uncomplimentary nickname "Dug-out Doug." In retrospect, while stationed in Manila, Corporal Zubrzycki pulled guard duty at General MacArthur's house. What miffed John was whenever they gave the General the proper recognition as an officer with a military salute, MacArthur never saluted in return, as was required by the Army.

On March 11, 1942, MacArthur was ordered by Washington, D.C. to leave the Philippine Islands. He slipped away through the Malinta Tunnel and got aboard a submarine which rendezvoused with a PT Boat that sped him on to Australia. As he was leaving, he vowed, "I shall return." Essentially, the troops were abandoned by their leader. The men had the sinking feeling that they were expendable. Major General Edward King and Major General Jonathan Wainwright were left in command. They were faced with a severe dearth of food, no fuel, and a shortage of viable ammunition. Meanwhile, Japanese forces were unrelenting in their ferocious attacks.

As a sidebar, the official Army record when John separated from the Army stated, *"Rifleman – Served with Company C, 31st Infantry in Philippine Islands. Was acting platoon sergeant of sixty-four men during the battle of Bataan Island. Deployed platoon in such a manner as to take best advantage of natural cover and in the positions which afforded maximum fire power on enemy forces. Used rifle, bayonet, and grenades to destroy enemy personnel. Assigned positions to men and acted on orders from platoon officer."*

The Japanese were a ruthless and formidable adversary. After four months of heroic fighting, the Battling Bastards of Bataan arrived at their date with destiny. The retreating American troops blew up their remaining ammunition supplies. The earth shook and the sky lit up from the barrage of explosions like the grand finale of a fireworks display back home.

It is estimated that 36,000 men died in the Battle of Bataan. Their souls were laid to rest as the remaining survivors had a horrific battle of survival still awaiting them.

Just prior to being surrendered, John was struggling to make his way back to the jungle hospital, being very ill from malaria. His body was already weak from having been grievously wounded in action just two and one-half months before. It was at this time that Maj. Gen. King gave orders to surrender. John was stopped in his tracks by the

Japanese as they gathered the captured men for a shakedown at Bataan Field.

While the men were assembled, John received a severe blow to the head as he was struck by one of the Japanese guards with a rifle butt. It knocked the WWI doughboy-style saucer helmet "clear off my head" and he believes the result was a concussion.

John was just one in a sea of totally defeated faces as all American and Filipino forces were ordered to lay down arms. The Battling Bastards of Bataan were surrendered to the Japanese invaders on April 9, 1942, and the infamous Bataan Death March began. Almost one month later, on May 5, 1942, Corregidor fell.

Major General Jonathan Wainwright composed his last message for President Roosevelt: *"With broken heart and head bowed in sadness but not in shame I report to your excellency that I must arrange terms for the surrender of the fortified islands of Manila Bay.*

There is a limit of human endurance and that limit has long since been past. Without prospect of relief I feel it is my duty to my country and to my gallant troops to end this useless effusion of blood and human sacrifice.

If you agree, Mr. President, please say to the nation that my troops and I have accomplished all that is humanly possible and that we have upheld the best traditions of the United States and its Army.

May God bless and preserve you and guide you and the nation in the effort to ultimate victory.

With profound regret and with continued pride in my gallant troops I go to meet the Japanese commander. Good-bye, Mr. President."

*"No Mama, no Papa, **no Uncle Sam**"*

Chapter 4

The Bataan Death March

This was the largest surrender of our troops in United States history. On April 9, 1942, the order to surrender was given by Major General Edward P. King, Jr. It was done as a humanitarian measure. He could not order his forces to fight to the death of the last man, knowing the result would be wholesale slaughter of his entire command. In their minds, the Battling Bastards of Bataan maintained that this was not "a surrender," but that they were "captured."

To the contrary, by the Japanese standard, such a gesture was seen as weakness and cowardice. Their Bushido Code of Conflict did not permit surrender. The Code states, "Do not survive to suffer the dishonor of capture." This Japanese field code ordained death over surrender, and a soldier was expected to save one round of ammo to commit suicide rather than be taken prisoner of war. In this way, he would not bring disgrace to his family or to his country.

The Japanese did not honor the Geneva Convention of 1929, signed by 47 nations governing the international conduct of war. Special provisions were made for the treatment of prisoners, but those rules of humane conduct were thrown out the window by the Americans' captors. The Japanese had been taught that they were a superior race. Those who surrendered and became prisoners of war were deemed subhuman--less worthy than dogs and to be treated as such, no-holds-barred.

On the Bataan Peninsula, these opposing cultures clashed and the unthinkable happened. The Japanese were on a rampage. An estimated 75,000 troops were surrendered: 60,000 Filipinos and 15,000 Americans. The Japanese anticipated only one-third that amount--about 25,000 men.

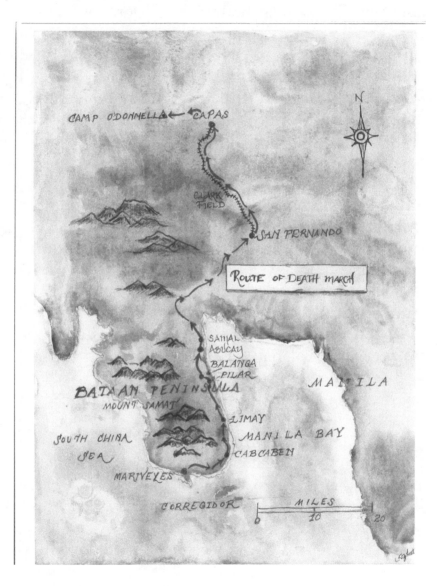

What became known as the infamous 'Bataan Death March' began. It was one of the most notorious atrocities in modern wartime history. The forced march from Mariveles at the southern end of the peninsula headed north to Camp

O'Donnell. It was approximately 70 miles, lasting five to six days. As the name implies, the Death March was just that. Prisoners died horrific deaths by the thousands, dying faster than they could be buried. Along the route, they were murdered by samurai sword and the bayonet, by gunshot and beatings, by torture, and starvation. Access to drinking water was not permitted and many died simply from dehydration and maddening thirst in the sweltering tropical heat. The men dropped like flies—thousands per day. Some 17,000 perished during the forced march. Estimates were that one out of every three prisoners died along the way.

If Sergeant John Zubrzycki only could opt to return to the "rough life" in Lackawanna of beatings, starving, and struggling that he sought to escape by joining the Army! It would have been a welcomed relief compared to what was to come after this surrender. When taken prisoner by enemy soldiers, he was very weak from his wounds, lack of food and rest, and overtaken by debilitating attacks of malaria. The malaria was causing him fever and chills as well as drifting in and out of consciousness. Add to that, the smashing blow to his head that came from the butt of a Japanese rifle and the odds looked impossibly long that the young US infantry sergeant would survive.

John was herded with the other prisoners into groups of 100 as they began to slog along the road for, what was to them, an unknown distance and an unknown duration. The sun was unforgiving as they marched slowly in the searing heat. The temperature in the tropics would climb to 120 degrees and the humidity was stifling. Most of the POWs were already sick, dazed, and delirious. Many with blistering mouths were overtaken by dysentery and malaria, marching in their own defecation. All were malnourished and exhausted. Most were given no water and many died of thirst. The Japanese overcame their captors like an all-consuming wild fire blazing out of control, intent on destroying anything or anyone in their way by any deplorable and inhumane method.

A rude awakening for the captives was to witness in total disbelief what they were seeing. Even though the men were suffering from dysentery as they marched in their own waste, they knew their fate if they dared to stop. If a prisoner stepped out of line from exhaustion or to relieve himself, he was bayoneted to death or beheaded! Heads were flying and blood was spurting from jugulars. The Japanese samurai sword, dazzling in the bright sun, came down like a flash of lightning. Swoosh! With a wide sweep, it separated heads from bodies. Horror rocked the marchers as they saw men beheaded directly before them. They secretly thought, "Will I be next?"

If you couldn't keep up, you were shot. If you fell out of line, you were bayoneted. Falling down was your death sentence. The march became a moving human slaughterhouse. Bodies of dead Filipinos and Americans lined both sides of the road. John recalls seeing Filipino civilians lined up along the road who would try to throw food to the marching column of starving men. Those Filipinos who were caught, including women and children, were bayoneted to death. The Japanese didn't want to "waste bullets," thus relying on their bayonets to deliver their fatal blows.

For five days, there was neither food nor water for the prisoners. Men who drank from the puddles of fetid, stagnant swamp water along the roadside paid dearly. These pools were wallows where carabao laid to keep cool and avoid biting insects. As a result, dysentery wreaked havoc among the prisoners. Some men were fortunate and quick enough to snatch up and devour banana peels that Japanese soldiers discarded in the dirt.

John saw plentiful artesian wells along the way that beckoned to the parched men. On occasion, the Japanese would come upon a lush waterfall and have the thirsty prisoners stand in front of it while denying them a drop of water. He saw crazed men break formation to run to the wells for just a drink of water, only to be mercilessly executed or clubbed to death. Many of those murders were carried out with glee and derision. Mercy was not a word in the Japanese vernacular.

John witnessed the regular bayoneting and beating to death of anyone who could not keep up in the march. At times, the Japanese would taunt a prisoner in the "spirit of fun," just to end up in beheading him as though it were a game. Beatings for no apparent reason and without provocation were commonplace. In some instances, staying alive was a matter of luck. A prisoner may have been spared being singled out at the whim of a sadistic Japanese soldier who whimsically imbedded his saber in the man's throat next to him, while laughing at his prey. The luckier prisoners were only poked and prodded with the end of a bayonet to keep them moving along.

John recalled that they stopped marching only one night. He was made to squat, not being allowed to sit, lie down, or even properly rest. The nights were very cold and the men shivered. On other days, they were required to squat in the noonday heat with the blazing sun beating down upon them as they baked in the oppressive heat. The POWs endured "sun treatment," being forced to look for hours directly toward the sun.

The line of tens of thousands of beleaguered men seemed endless, stretching en masse as far as the eye could see. Sounds of groaning men, with boots shuffling along the dusty road kicking up billows of dirt, found time measured in steps. One day mercilessly blended into another day and then another. Dust filled the nostrils, mouths were parched, deliria dimming their minds as Hell itself reared its ugly head.

Seemingly endless acts of cruelty continued as well. Along the Death March, there were crucified prisoners. The bodies of these men were literally impaled with bayonets that pierced their throats, hands, and feet. To underscore the sadistic mindset of their captors, a vivid memory was tattooed on the minds of the marchers. A prisoner who was stumbling and wavering was taken by the arm by a Japanese soldier and lead into the middle of the road. What was approaching was a Japanese convoy and the prisoner was crushed and run over continuously by trucks and tanks. Remaining was only an imprint of what moments ago was a human being. The victim was completely flattened, like the metaphorical pancake, with only an outline of his clothing as evidence he ever lived. But this was no metaphor.

As some men staggered and no longer able to walk on their own, their comrades would come to their aid, holding them up while the weak slung their arms over the shoulders of another marcher. Others who were too ill to walk were carried in makeshift first aid litters—a blanket pulled tightly between two poles as the stronger men carried almost lifeless bodies that sagged in the blanket. While in a shocked stupor and state of delirium, John was struggling to put one foot in front of the other. Two comrades held him up as they painfully trudged on along the dusty road covered by the stench of death and human excrement. John said he doesn't think he could have made it another mile, but recalled someone calling out, "Hang in there. We are almost there. You're going to make it." John said, "If you couldn't make it, you were executed.   I just had *the will to survive*."

Finally, after what seemed like an eternity, the first leg of the march ended at San Fernando.   But the suffering wasn't over.   Here, the prisoners were herded into filthy, penned-in livestock enclosures before being loaded into small box cars standing on the adjacent railway.   Men were jammed into these box cars that had become excruciatingly hot ovens from the intense tropical sun.   The foul smell and heat were overwhelming.   The POWs were fainting and suffocating while in a standing position. Others met their death while still upright on their feet, being packed so tightly into these cars.   There was no place to fall. The rail cars, which could typically carry 30 to 40 people were now crammed with 100.   The 15-mile train ride ended in a town called Capas, but after disembarking, they still had to march another six miles to Camp O'Donnell. Anywhere from an estimated 50,000 to 54,000 men made it to the converted camp which had a capacity to accommodate just 8,000.

Conditions at the camp were utterly deplorable.   So many POWs had dysentery with no control over their bowels, that human waste covered everything.   There was nothing else to do but just sit, squat, or lie down in excrement.   Every surface of everything, including the men, was covered with millions of disease-carrying flies.

Having been deprived of something as fundamental and necessary as water, John recalled a particularly torturing incident.   They were all made to sit "at attention" in the hot sun of an unshaded parade field.   Before them was a plumbing spigot that was dripping water and all eyes were glued upon it.   The cruelty was that they were not permitted even one drop of the life-saving water upon penalty of death should they lose all sanity, break formation, and make a rush for that tempting, dripping spigot.

Those who were able were assigned to burial detail. Some POWs would dig the mass graves and the others would carry the bodies. The corpses stunk in the heat and they tried to put the bodies that had been dead the longest into the graves first. Trying to put twenty bodies into each hole, they were arranged in such a way as to keep them straight and make enough room, at times stacked two deep. Some familiar faces were recognized as friends buried friends. One POW who was on burial detail would later bury his own brother.

Many on the burial detail literally dropped dead from exhaustion and overwork while performing their duties. They were simply and unceremoniously thrown into the mass graves they had been digging for their fallen comrades. Even more ghastly were the times when men who collapsed from exhaustion but were still alive were ordered to be dumped into the grave—buried alive, screaming with their hands reaching out for help. Besides men who were buried alive, some were forced to dig their own graves before being executed.

Twice as many Americans died in the first two months in prison camp at O'Donnell than had died on the Death March. The camp had become a massive graveyard. With the simplest care of proper medical attention, hydration, and drugs, the horrible debilitating disease of dysentery could have been controlled. But the Japanese, with their indifference toward the suffering men, preferred to allow the POWs to perish. Zubrzycki's commanding officer, Captain Carnahan, was among the thousands of victims. Having survived the Battle of Bataan and the Death March, it was dysentery that led to his untimely demise. On May 10, 1942, the Captain died in this cesspool of a camp.

In June, 1942, the men, including John, were marched northeast from Camp O'Donnell to the prison camp Cabanatuan. This camp was also overcrowded with unsanitary, spartan conditions and the men slept on lice-infested bamboo straw mats. Rats were abundant. They were incessantly being attacked by bugs and hordes of flies. Again, their mantra was sounded, "Who die, you or the fly." Killing flies became not only a pastime but a necessity. John said it was also a "mosquito factory." The dead bodies were left lying around and the horrific stench was nauseating.

It is here that John was on the brink of death once again and that terrifying specter stared him in the face. Fading into a state of unconsciousness, he was placed in what was called the "Zero Ward" of a makeshift hospital. The next ward was called the "Saint Peter's Ward," which was the morgue. The sickest of the POWs were in the "Zero Ward," so named because you had a "zero chance" of making it out alive. And very few did make it out alive. It was a gruesome place where maggots were seen eating the rotten flesh in open wounds of some of those who were teetering on death's doorstep.

A fellow soldier spoon fed John for three days while he was in a coma. And another unidentified POW tried to ease John's fever from the malaria that was "burning him up" by wiping his forehead and lips with a damp cloth. When he recovered consciousness, he stayed next to a sewage trench for quite some time because of the strong urge to defecate due to dysentery. John's number wasn't up and he miraculously pulled through once again. Over the next several months his strength slowly started to return.

John would say, "When you got your daily meager portion of rice, it was best to close your eyes while eating since the rice 'moved' from the maggots crawling in your food. There were just too many worms to be picked out." Rice was often floor sweepings that contained dirt and fine gravel. Meat was issued in minute portions, anywhere from one quarter ounce to one ounce per man, per week. At times, the meat was either putrid or decomposed.

The men all looked out for one another and offered comfort to the very ill. It was during John's confinement in Cabanatuan that he held an older career soldier from "C" Company in his arms as the man passed away. Cradling his comrade in his arms, he had to wonder with eyes glazing over who will be next as he mourned this loss of his friend's life. Approximately half of the 1600 members of the 31st Infantry "Polar Bear" regiment who were surrendered at Bataan died while they were prisoners of war.

Man on left later died in John's arms (Photo credit: American Ex-Prisoners of War)

In one incident, knowing he was putting his life at risk, John escaped out of the camp to get medical supplies that he learned were hidden by the Army medics. Utilizing a drainage ditch that ran beneath the barbed-wire fence, he then sneaked back into camp to bring those supplies to his fellow comrades. He said, "I got some quinine and sulfur (sulfanilamides – internal germicide drugs). It came in handy to help your buddies that got sick."

In Cabanatuan, three officers who tried to escape were caught. The Japanese stripped them, tied them to a post in front of the camp gate, and forced passing Filipinos to beat them across the face with a 2 x 4 board. The officers were kept in the scorching sun for two days without water. Finally, one was beheaded and the other two were shot. The message delivered was very clear as to the fate for anyone contemplating escape.

Three prisoners beaten with clubs (Photo credit: American Ex-Prisoners of War)

John spent four months in Cabanatuan before being transferred at the beginning of October, 1942, to Bilibid Prison. A doctor suggested to John he had better get out of Cabanatuan, since the Japanese were looking for an additional workforce of skilled trades. His fellow prisoners encouraged him to volunteer for this workforce because he would surely die if he stayed at the camp. As a result, John volunteered to go on a ship to Manchuria, China.

Bilibid, located on the Manila Bay, was a federal prison during peacetime. Now, it served as a clearinghouse for transferring prisoners to other camps. While in Bilibid, John slept on a cold concrete floor. All prisoners were required to bow down to any Japanese soldier, regardless of rank. When John refused to bow, the result was a very severe beating. Along with the other prisoners, he reluctantly learned that resistance of any kind would not be tolerated by their ruthless captors.

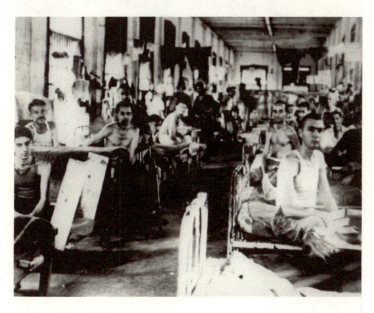

Bilibid POW hospital ward (Photo credit: American Ex-Prisoners of War)

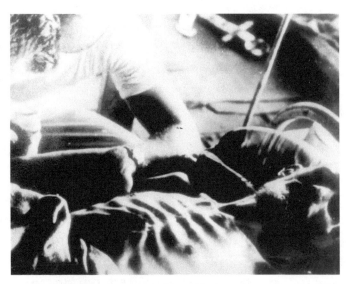

An American POW suffering from dry beri-beri in
Bilibid (Photo credit: American Ex-Prisoners of War)

San Tomas prison camp in Manila; internees Lee Rogers and
John Todd (Photo credit: American Ex-Prisoners of War

Anxious to get out of Cabanatuan and Bilibid, on October 8, 1942, he was marched to a loading dock to be shipped out of Manila Bay on a Japanese freighter. Here, it was six months after he was surrendered on April 9, 1942, and he was still wearing the same filthy, frayed clothes. Walking down the gang plank, John had only a "snapshot" moment as he glanced at the beauty of the bay. Thoughts flashed back to the once pleasant memories when he first arrived on the Islands. He could not have possibly imagined the horrors that were about to befall him. After the war, he would say, "The Bataan Death March was a picnic compared to the Hell Ships."

*"No Mama, no Papa, **no Uncle Sam**"*

Sgt. Zubrzycki obtained a journal at some point during his internment. These poems are from his notes and appear exactly as it is in his journal. (The words "dysentry maru" refers to the Hell Ship.)

GOODBYE BATAAN

**THERES A TRANSPORT JUST LEAVING LUZON
GOODBYE TO THE FALL OF BATAAN
THE BATTLE IS OVER & WE MIGHT NOT HAVE WON
BUT WE'LL SEE THE DEFEAT OF NIPPON.**

**WE SAILED ON THE DYSENTRY MARU
I THOUGHT I'D BE BURIED IN THE BLUE
WITH STOUT HEARTHS & CHEER & YANKS EVER NEAR
I KNOW WE'LL SEE THIS THING TROUGH.**

SO BOYS LET US EAT ALL OUR MAIZE

FOR TOMORROW WHO KNOWS WE MAY GAZE
ON A TRANSPORT ANEW FLYING THE RED-WHITE &
BLUE
SO CHEER UP MY LADS WE'RE NOT THROUGH.

SAY A PRAYER FOR THE BOYS WHO ARE NOT HERE
THEY DIED FACING JAPS WITH A SNEER
WE SALUTE THOSE DEAR LADS
THERE THE BEST TO BE HAD.

*   *   *

LEST WE FORGET

WHEN I SIT DOWN TO THINK
MY MIND GOES ON THE BLINK
I CAN'T REMEMBER MEN NOR PLACES THAT I HAVE
BEEN
A FAMILIAR FACE OFTEN LOOKS OUT OF PLACE
THEN I BEGIN TO WONDER
IF MY MENTAL STATE WAS FIRST A GIFT
SO THAT I MIGHT NEVER RECALL
BATAAN AND CORREGIDOR'S UNHAPPY FALL.

Chapter 5

The Hell Ships – Standing Room Only

Months of combat--Wounded in action--The Bataan Death March--Crammed   San Fernando boxcars--Camp O'Donnell--Cabanatuan's   Zero   Ward--Bilibid   Prison. There is just no way that conditions could conceivably get worse.   As mentioned earlier, Sergeant Zubrzycki said, "The Death March was a picnic compared to the Hell Ships." The agony he endured was a tiresomely perpetual continuum of various facets of man's inhumanity to man.

With the ongoing war effort, between 1942 and 1945, the Japanese needed to replenish their labor force. The least sickly of the prisoners were recruited to be shipped by ocean freighters to various camps in Japan and China.   Dozens of these ships transported thousands of POWs to mines and industrial sites where they were to be used as slave labor.   All Japanese merchant ship names were followed by the word "Maru," meaning "circle" in Japanese.

John and other POWs were herded like cattle onto the freighter called the *Tottori Maru* that departed Manila on October 8, 1942.   Gripping the metal ladder as he slowly made his way down the steps into the hold, his first thought was to stake out his claim for a bunk.   What a mistake.   That wasn't going to work as more and more men descended the ladder taking up every available inch of space.   He said, "I was one of the unfortunate guys being placed in the bottom of the ship's hold, thinking I would pick out a place to stay.   I was quickly beaten up by my fellow prisoners who wanted my space as we were being crammed into this small hold. There was no air and we were suffocating. There were 1200 men jammed in an area meant for only 200."

They were crowded in so tightly that there was barely room to even move, yet the Japanese were still trying to force more men into the hold. They shouted at them to pack tighter together with total disregard for any measure of humane treatment.

From the outset, the *Tottori Maru* (with two holds designated for prisoners) also had on board POWs from Mindanao and Luzon, bringing the total of POWs to 1,992. In addition, several hundred enemy soldiers were boarded on this transport, with the top decks and two additional holds reserved for the Japanese.

Some of the more fortunate POWs who could not be squished into the holds remained on deck where there was air to breathe. There were primitive latrines that hung over the sides of the ship for those who were in a strategic position to use them. Only those POWs in the hold who were closest to the ladder had limited access to the top-side to use these latrines at the discretion of a Japanese guard. All the others had no such luck.

The "Hell Ships" were aptly named by the POWs. Conditions were abysmal. When the men entered these cargo holds, they plummeted into the bowels of Hell. They were crammed in tighter than sardines in a can—vertical, not horizontal, sardines. John said, "The sardines had it better because at least they were dead, but we were still alive. There was no room to lie down and you either squatted or stood." This went on for 30 days as the freighter made its 1600-mile journey. At times, POWs would become hauntingly aware that the GI they stood next to was unresponsive, just a corpse in an upright position with no room to fall down. The foul, gagging odor of the decomposing bodies in the stifling heat and humidity of the hold saturated what scarce air there was. The groaning emitted from hopelessly ill men was incessant. The ship may as well have been a floating coffin. Eventually, those who perished were passed up to the Japanese, tossed overboard, and unceremoniously buried at sea. These deaths sadly now made a bit more room for the survivors still enduring their macabre, living nightmare.

Those were not the only troubles. Can the reader imagine--torpedoes! The Japanese freighters were not marked to indicate that American POWs were onboard. On October 9, American submarines that were hunting targets in the South China Sea started to fire at these ships. One submarine, the "SS Grenadier" set sights on a ship and fired away. A Japanese skipper warned that torpedoes were coming toward the *Tottori Maru*! The captain saw them coming—the two torpedoes that were fired, skimming just under the surface of the water. The captain reacted immediately and abruptly turned the ship causing the torpedoes to go past the stern. John said they could hear these underwater missiles whizzing past them, missing their target. Some of the Hell Ships were hit and all perished on those transports. Approximately 4,000 to 5,000 American POWs died in those ships that were sunk. John said, "The guys who got hit were the lucky ones. Some men were praying to God that they be hit, too. It would have been better if our ship had been torpedoed rather than to have to live through this." Death would have been a welcomed relief from being in this floating cesspool. The Hell Ships continued onward in a convoy of about 14 freighters.

Those of us who have never been forced to undergo such fiendish deprivation can never fully grasp the incomprehensible. These men were living like animals and had to make every effort to survive another day. Every hour of every day was a sheer struggle to stay alive. According to John, it became "every man for himself." We can only imagine what hell must be like. In holds where no humans should have entered, the POWs in the holds of the *Tottori Maru* were literally living in hell.

It was the overwhelming smell of death that gravely affected those in the depths of this dark abyss. With the deprivation of air, the men were being asphyxiated from the stomach churning stench. Besides the decomposing bodies, the putrid air was rank with human excrement, urine, sweat, and vomit from sea sickness as the temperatures rose to a stifling 100 degrees or more. There were no fans or ventilation to breathe life-sustaining oxygen into the below-deck compartments and there was also no provision for adequate light. Many of the traumatized POWs became hysterical as they stood teetering in a stark pall of maddening darkness and despair.

All the men were covered from head to toe with lice. In this pit of darkness John could feel the lice squirming on every inch of his skin. They were a grim reminder that he must still be alive if he was able to detect this crawling sensation. Later he would jokingly say, "It was infested really bad with lice. There were so many lice that they were what kept the ship afloat." Later it was learned that these cargo holds previously carried horses and other animals which added another layer to the filth and odor.

A five-gallon bucket of either food or water and a bucket for human waste would be lowered through the opened hatch door. As John would gingerly pick his way in the dim light through the throngs of starving men toward the bucket, he would wonder what unidentifiable slop awaited them this time. They were fed exceedingly meager portions of a small ball of rice or crackers and some sips of water. He said, "There was never enough food to reach the bottom of the pile of men. It was like one hot dog distributed to a packed arena. And the bucket that was sent down for your urine and excrement didn't work and it was a mess. You can't even visualize it. You cannot even picture it." The men with dysentery literally defecated right where they stood and so, directly upon one another. The sloppy mess created by uncontrollable bowels was infinitely worse than the conditions at Camp O'Donnell or Cabanatuan and the men referred to the *Tottori Maru* as the "Diarrhea Maru."

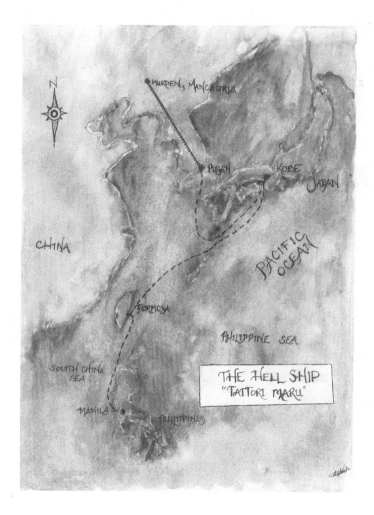

On October 11, 1942, the *Tottori Maru* made a stop in Formosa, known today as Taiwan, to take on fuel. The prisoners were unloaded onto the dock, stripped naked, and hosed down with a fire hose to remove the caked-on filth and lice that infested their bodies. There were people on the loading docks--women carrying baskets of coal, among others. It was very humiliating for the men as they stood there naked, just skin and bones, deliberately put on public display, before being herded back on to the freighter. John's one memory of Formosa is that he ate a grapefruit, skin and all. For an ever so brief moment, it felt as though the POWs casket was opened and they came alive. Feeling the cool breeze on their flesh, inhaling fresh air, and being in the pure, streaming sunlight was but a short-lived dream. Back in the hold, the Gates of Hell slammed shut once again. The departure from Formosa was delayed several days with the arrival of a typhoon. Then the ship was having mechanical troubles, causing further delays. It was near the end of October when the *Tottori Maru* finally left Formosa.

These shadows of human form, these forsaken victims, were living a nightmare and they lost touch with their humanity. Men were losing their minds and becoming totally deranged. The hideously unnerving sounds of their blood-curdling shrieking and screaming from going mad would never be removed from the POWs minds. Suffering from extreme thirst and hunger for so long, they trampled one another if there was any food or water to be had, even killing for it. From lack of water, they were licking the condensation that ran down the steel walls of the ship from high humidity. Some men were drinking urine. How could anyone retain any semblance of sanity in that small, cramped den of bedlam? As they journeyed in this unceasingly timeless void, there was not even a flicker of hope on the horizon of time. They were crossing The River Styx, and Charon (the mythological ferryman) was collecting his fare in complete, dehumanizing control.

At one point, total chaos broke out. Apparently, one prisoner's animal instincts turned to cannibalism, driven mad by hunger and thirst. He grabbed a man next to him and cut his arms to drink his blood. When two other guys nearby realized what was happening, they pulled the crazed man off his prey and beat him to death. None too soon, this gruesome journey would be over for these weary and broken men.

They made another stopover in Kobe, Japan, to unload a group of POWS and the crazed, 30-day departure from reality in the ship's hold finally ended on November 8, 1942, when the *Tottori Maru* docked in Pusan on the Choson Peninsula of Korea. The Japanese called the city 'Fusan' and it was also referred to as 'Busan.' While disembarking, John said it was very cold and his emaciated, boney body was turning purple. The temperature had dropped drastically since leaving the tropics as their bodies now shivered in threadbare, tattered clothes.

The next day, the ragged mass of men were marched to a train station, where they were given a boxed lunch of what John described as, "Pretty decent food consisting of rice and a relish or sweet type of pickle." Once again, they were herded en masse and loaded on a train, still covered with the hitchhiking lice that were unwanted, yet familiar traveling companions. The doors shut and the weary POWs journeyed by rail for two days from Korea to northeast China. Destination: Manchuria.

From John Zubrzycki's journal, copied in pencil in his own handwriting, presumably from another POWs journal, is a detailed account of the Hell Ship *"Oryoku*

Maru." The account begins on December 13, 1944, two years after John's journey on the *Tottori Maru.*

"Journal of trip from Manila to Japan"
Started to leave Billibid prison shortly after 8:00 A.M. **Dec.13, 1944**. Turned back because of air raid, left 11:30 A.M. Sat on pier 7 most of the afternoon watching Japs (civilians??) troops and merchant marine being loaded aboard mostly women and children, Port area quite damaged by previous bombings, observed many troops cavalry being unloaded from transports. Boarded **"ORYOKU" MARU** 1649 officers & enlisted men including about 30 British & Dutch. Received 3/4 canteen cup of steamed rice 1/8 cup soup, no water, very hot & sultry. Bombed all day between Manila & Subic Bay by U.S. Navy dive bombers on Dec. 14 from 9:00 A.M. to dusk. I received one wound & scratches at 4:00 P.M. on right hip, received 3/4 cup rice 1/8 cup soup no water. That night extremely hot in hold many passing out including myself due to lack of air & water. Many men went crazy & started to kill other men. Had to kill them for self protection no sleep that night, more like a nightmare. I don't know how many men were killed, but I hope I never experience another night. Civilians were unloaded during that night. Dec 15 ship was bombed & hit. Lucky for us we were in Subic Bay & shallow waters ship sunk & sat on bottom of shallow water 10:00 A.M. direct hit on after hold our hold filled with smoke & fumes from bomb men made rush for ladders & nip guards fired rifles into hold killing many. Permission was given to abandon ship Col. Wilson several other men & myself tried to rescue several injured men pinned under debris. Very weak & hold full of smoke & fumes from bomb & also fire. Worked at this until had to leave due to excessive heat. Reached to deck saw many of our men ransacking a Jap galley I joined in the procession until Jap guard began to shoot at us, Dove overboard in nothing but G-string, Left many men in hold who apparently died or perished with the ship. U.S. planes returned but did not fire on us after recognizing men already on beach All men were congregated into tennis court watched U.S. planes finish bombing ORYOKO MARU & Jap installations on shore. Received no food and little water. Dec. 16, 44-- 1333 survivors ashore out of 1619. No clothes, tired, hot sun, no food. 9 U.S. Dive Bomb (stroffed??) & bombed OLANGAPO AREA several men injured from bomb fragments. Dec.

17, 44 (Sun??) terrific, 4 deaths 2 1/2 G.I. spoons of dry rice thank God we could get water Dec. 18, 44 (Some.??) Dec. 19, 44 men getting weak hardly can walk scorched by sun during day & freezing at night 4 spoons dry rice & lots of water (almost a ??bony___?)

Dec. 20 - 44, 4 1/2 days at tennis court received total 13 1/2 spoons dry rice 681 men moved to jail in San Fernando (Pompang??) 4 spoons dry rice

Dec. 21 - 44 at San Fernando 2 meals total 125 grams steamed rice

Dec. 22 - 44   300 grams steamed rice.   Rest of men from Olangapo arrived Still suffering from sun & cold nights (exposure)

Dec. 23 -44 300 grams rice Rumor of move to Billibid 1/5 sick & wounded moved to Billibid

Dec. 24 -44 Awakened at 3:00 A.M. to be moved to San Fernando La (Univ?) 170 men to boxcar No food or water Air raid while being loaded Arrived at San Fernando about 3:00 A.M.

 Dec. 25 What a way to spend Xmas no food no water or clothes Slept on Station platform all day everyone filthy & dead tired from lack of food & no water

Dec. 25 - 44 moved to school yard very hard to walk on street with bare feet. Received 2 meals of steamed rice (1/2 cup rice 1/2 cup water) Moved to beach about 9:00 A.M. That ended Xmas day one I shall always remember

Dec. 26 - 44 Standing by on beach (sand dunes) waiting for another trip 5 spoons of water & one small rice ball

Dec. 27 - 44 boarded large horse transport stole some barley from (barge?) got underway in morning, 2nd air raid in P.M. Ships not hit 1 meal of 1/2 cup steamed & 1/2 cup of warm tea 2nd Lt. D.C. shot while attempting to escape. Convoy consisted of 2 destroyers & 3 freighters

Dec. 28 - 44 1/3 cup of rice & small piece of fish 1/3 cup of tea in A.M. getting cooler.   Passed another end of Luzon at 2:00 P.M. plenty of air short on water & clothes, very crowded sitting room only necessary to stretch out in relays Submarine attack 3 torpedoes fired at us but missed

Dec. 29 - 44 1/3 cup rice no water air raid

Dec. 30 - 44 1/3 cup steamed rice 5 spoons of soup 1/3 cup water

Dec. 31 -44 Arrived at TAKAO 1/2 cup rice

Jan. 1 - 45 New Years day aboard ship in harbor 2 meals of 1/2 cup rice flies horrible men sick & dying of Dysentery & starvation no water

Jan. 2 - 45 1/3 cup rice 1/3 cup water

Jan. 3. Air raid in A.M. 3 spoons of dry rice 1/3 cup steamed rice 1/4 cup soup 1 cup water Big celebration

Jan. 4 1 meal with little rice & soup 34 dead since Olongapo

Jan. 5. 1/2 cup rice 1/8 cup water

Jan. 6 All day loading sugar 1/2 cup rice 1/2 cup water.

Jan. 7 2 small meals of rice 5 G.I. spoons H2O

Jan. 8 Still in TAKAO HARBOR men broke into lower hold for sugar Japs gave warning to shoot filled my belly with sugar

Jan. 9 Sent Dutch and Br. to P.O.W. camp about noon we were hit by 5 bombers 2 direct hits in forward hold 2 direct hits in rear hold many wounded, I received 2 more wounds men stealing sugar many dying.

Jan. 10 2 meals 1/4 cup water no med for wounded.

Jan. 11 cleaned dead out of hold after a few nights. Small group of Red Cross Japs came aboard dressed some mens wounds. Seemed to be great support (or sport?) 224 killed out of 473 in forward hold many in rear hold. 5 cases of DEPHTERIA (sic), lot of Dysentery many flies smell putrid much suffering

Jan. 12 Very cold night still no clothes as soon as man dies clothes are removed & fought for ship is aground

Jan. 13 moved to another freighter 1 small meal of steamed rice no water men going nuts for water

Jan. 14 Moved out to sea in convoy no water bottom hold filled with sugar managed to get some

Jan. 15 2 meals dry rice 1 teaspoon of salty (miza?) paste no water men dying of starvation thirst unattended wounds allmost (sic) all who had (---?) wounds contracted g---? ganrene odor unbearable my wounds sore but not infected

Jan. 16 extremely cold no clothes no shoes lost my buddy who died this morning from wounds in the guts

Jan 17 32 died today very little water

Jan. 18 2 light meals 1/8 cup water

Jan. 19 " " " 1/4 " "

" 20 Men dying 30 per day

Jan. 21 2 meals rice 1/8 cup water men dying

Jan. 22 " " " " "

Jan. 23 Snowing today still no clothes

Jan. 24 Very cold still dying almost 30 per day Snow hard on feet

Jan. 25 Cold as hell men dying 2 meals

Jan 26 Anchored 4 hrs. last night (---?) three large groups of (-----?) 2 meals no water

Jan. 27 Anchored all day 1 meal 1/8 cup

Jan. 28 deaths increasing sailing 6:00 A.M.

Jan. 29   Attacked by cubs(?)   missed us during night depth charges dropped anchored about dawn

 2 meals little water Roll call of survivors 497 out of original 1619 + 7 = 1626 inspected by many Jap officers

Jan. 30 Issued clothes disembarked at Moji , KUS-SHU Japan divided in 4 groups My group sick and wounded 110 men moji Hosp. was given mattress filled with sawdust 6 blankets slept on floor just like in Heaven rooms cold as ice no heaters

Feb. 1 - 45 Got the runs crapped in bed having tough time keeping chow in the gut 1 bowl rice 1/2 cup soup & 1/2 cup tea for all day.

Chapter 6

Mukden POW Camp

The cloaked Grim Reaper, with black hood covering his bent head and scythe raised high, gazed upon the ghastly forms of prisoners of war who were disembarking the *Tottori Maru*. How many will succumb in the next arena of the survival of the fittest? It was a heinous sight--those men with haggard countenances, who had thus far defied death and the vilest of treatment, and who were finally vomited out of the holds of the Hell Ship.

Just 30 days earlier, they were in the stifling heat of the tropics. Now, on November 11, 1942, the train ride terminated where the snow-covered ground sparkled in the sunlight. The sound of the cold crunched underfoot. Seeing their breath upon each exhale, the frigid air nipped at their skin. By some miracle, warmer clothes were issued to the mangy semblances of human beings. The barefooted men were given shoes that helped to brace against the falling temperatures.

A stiff, bone-chilling wind was blowing unceasingly and the gaunt men shivered. John's eyes quickly darted about, carefully surveying his surroundings which were to become his home for the next three years. His sharp blue eyes now looked at life through a veiled lens that sought only resources necessary for survival.

Where had destiny brought them now? The chronologically young, but physically aged, Sergeant Zubrzycki ended up in Japanese-held Manchuria in Northeastern China. By fate, this young man from Lackawanna was still alive, defying the odds that death surely should have come by now. Leaving the train, the

Americans were joined by British and Australian POWs and marched to a barbed wire-enclosed camp about a mile north of a city called Mukden. Today the city is known as Shenyang. Later, in July of 1943, new two-story barracks would be built to accommodate the POWs. Camp 2 was surrounded by a brick wall manned by guards 24/7. The Japanese referred to it as Camp Hoten.

This area of Manchuria was also called Manchukuo, from the factory named Manchukuo Kabushiki Kaisha (MKK), where several of the POWs were put to work. By conjecture, it was believed that Henry Ford had some part in the building of MKK prior to the war. Soybeans were widely cultivated in Manchuria and the nearby Manchurian Soybean Industry, Co. was the only plant worldwide that devised a way for commercial soybean extraction using a solvent other than the petroleum variety. Henry Ford was actively researching the use of synthetic plastics made with soybeans to manufacture car parts. The POWs who were working in the MKK plant found equipment for making Ford parts in large crates that were shipped from the United States. Along with this, they found Ford Motor Company paperwork. It was inferred from this evidence found by the POWs that the plan to manufacture car parts here in China was abandoned due to the outbreak of the war.

The initial barracks that would house the POWs was in Camp 1, made up of primitive low buildings, half-buried under the ground. These barracks built at the time of the Russo-Japanese War did not provide adequate shelter due to the severity of the winter. Being three steps down from ground level, they were designed to supposedly provide insulation against the cold, arctic-like climate. Well, only in theory, that is. The men were extremely emaciated from being interned at Cabanatuan, followed by the journey on the Hell Ship. Their health had deteriorated significantly.   Upon arrival, each man was issued six blankets as the temperature plummeted to well below-zero.

Within the barracks, the men slept on a raised wooden platform that was about six inches off the ground. Many of the men, including John, were suffering from beriberi, a painful disease, which caused their feet to be inflamed and a feeling that they were burning up. At night, John would hang his feet off the wooden platform in an effort to cool them. When a guard passed and noticed John's feet, he took his rifle butt and struck his feet, smashing them repeatedly. From there on out, he would have to hold his legs in so that his feet would not be beaten or broken.

He later recounted that he found a way to loosen the nails in the wooden planks in the barracks and could lift up some of the boards. "I figured out where I could hide out when the time came. At the end of the war, they were going to annihilate all the POWs and I could hide out under the platform or in a manhole."

Japanese barracks in background and Japanese administrative building in foreground

Top photo: Barracks in background and parade ground in foreground
Bottom photo: Half of a sleeping alcove for 32 men and eight men per bunk. There were five alcoves on each side

That first dismal winter, almost 200 of the 1,494 POWs died—most of them during the first few months after arriving at Mukden. The bodies were simply piled on top of one another in a warehouse like logs in a pile of timber. The clothes would be removed from the corpses and the POWs took the clothes for themselves for extra warmth. These unfortunate souls were in "cold storage," awaiting the spring thaw because the cruel ground was too frozen and not receptive to receiving their remains.

John believed that having lived through the four seasons of Western New York aided in his survival of the brutal winters in China. "They did not issue us proper winter clothing and I remember the water freezing inside of my canteen. When I was at Camp 1, that first winter, guys were dying of pneumonia and dysentery. We had intestinal worms and fungal infections.

"There was no heat in the barracks, but some heat was rationed. You had a bucket of coal and a bundle of kindling and the fire lasted maybe one or two hours. It was 30 below to 40 below-zero in Mukden and it was hard to breathe in the cold weather. Frost formed on the inside walls of the barracks. We were given old coats that had what looked like bullet holes in them and footwear. At first, before it became cold, we only had open 'wooden clogs' for our feet. When the weather got more severe, we were given blankets. But by a certain date, regardless if it was still cold out, we had to turn in the blankets and coats.

"We were always getting called out for roll call regardless of how cold it was. One time in particular, they had us strip naked and threw cold water on us, making us stand at attention in the freezing weather." The weather was bitterly cold during the very long winters in Manchuria. With the unforgiving cold piercing down to the marrow of his bones, John stuffed straw into his clothes to provide a little more insulation. It was likened to entering a walk-in freezer at a meat packing plant, but there certainly was no meat to be found on the bones of these walking skeletons of men. Having been systematically starved for over seven months, John's weight dropped to under 90 pounds.

Each POW was assigned a number and they were expected to learn to count in Japanese in short order. The first day, they were to learn to count from one to 50: ichi, ni, san, shi, go, roku, shichi, hachi, kyu, ju…….The second day, they had to count from 50 to 100. John said, "We had roll call on a daily basis, saying our number in Japanese. My number was **433**. During one roll call, I got the number wrong and the guard removed his shoe and kept beating me across the mouth. " Chillingly, the number **433** became his identity and would stay with John for the next 70 years of his life.

Mukden Roster lists "433 Zubrzycki, John"

Life at Mukden was bleak at best. With slumped shoulders and faces full of despair, the men were reduced to "survival mode." The conversations among the men were always about food and different recipes. Their hunger gave them a constant gnawing pain. Any chance to steal food was always on their internal radar screen. John said, "I was

73

always plotting how to get food, all the time knowing if I got caught it would result in a severe beating. It was worth getting the beating if you could at least get some extra food."

Sure enough, like a hungry animal stalking its prey and crossing the grounds while on a work detail, John's eye caught the sight of an open bag that was leaking brown sugar. He was with several other POWs who also conspired on this opportunity. Lunging for this sweet pile of goodness, he crammed a handful into his famished mouth. Then it happened. Being caught red-handed with a face full of sugar, a guard was to unleash his madness. John recounted this event, recalling the name of one brutal guard, Lt. Ineo Kasma. "I stole some extra food with several other men and was caught. For four days, I was either being beaten unconscious or in the guardhouse because I wouldn't tell who the other men were. They started by using a shoe to hit me in the face and, after that, a bamboo pole." The harsh punishment hardly fit the crime.

Every meal eaten in Mukden was soup. In the morning before marching to work, the soup would be served from a wooden bucket and each man got one dipper-full, which was mainly cornmeal or maize from soy beans. In the fall, there were more vegetables, but most of it was rotten potatoes. Rotten potato soup. There was rarely any meat and if such a microscopic serving could be detected it was the size of a fingernail. Obtaining food was all-consuming as the POWs would even steal food from each other. With every man for himself, the men became unable to even trust each other at this point. Fights among the men over food were common. When it was a prisoner's turn to dish out the soup, he often would put the dipper down to the bottom of the pot where there was a small amount of food versus only broth and give more food to his buddies. One saving grace was the availability of garlic. This revered bulb had antibacterial properties and other health benefits.

Then there were the stray dogs that were unfortunate enough to wander under the barbed wire fence into the camp. Taking advantage of these four-legged walking meals, the men fashioned various materials into ropes which were then utilized to catch the dogs. John said, "The dumb dogs got into camp by mistake. We would beat them and skin them. A buddy by the name of Jack Williams knew how to cut up the dog meat and find the filet portion. Jack and I saved the dog tenderloin for ourselves as our bonus for killing the dog. We would put the meat in with the pot of soup. One guy refused to eat the dog meat and he died the next day. We would find sparrows and vermin to supplement our food. Then we would trade the skinned dog fur with the Chinese for cigarettes." Eventually, this dog-trapping scheme lead to a paucity of strays in the area!

Every year on April 29, as an act of 'largesse,' the men would get the day off from laboring in honor of Japanese Emperor Hirohito's birthday. As a gift, each man was given one orange, which was extolled as an "act of his highness' generosity." What irony that was! Starve and beat the men all year long, then give them an orange on one special day.

The Trans-Siberian Railroad network included a connecting branch with the Trans-Manchurian line and the South Manchurian Railway. The proximity of this vast railroad system lent the area surrounding Mukden favorable to various manufacturing facilities in this huge industrial complex. The POWs were recruited as slave labor to work at these factories to aid the Japanese war effort. In addition, the poor lower-class of local Chinese were working both inside these factories and on the outside hauling goods to and from.

Surrounding the temporary Camp 1 were satellite camps, where the men slaved at work. These included coal mines, copper mines, a tool and die factory, a textile factory that made twine to be used to make canvass at the textile mill, logging, farming, and working on the nearby railroads.

John was in close proximity to the Great Wall of China that was built during the Ming Dynasty. He said, "They had me chipping mortar off the stones and bricks of the Great Wall from dawn to dusk before transferring me to a factory."

The men would be awakened in the dark winter mornings and sent off to work. John was now assigned to a textile factory where he made canvass. Six days a week, he made the five-mile march each way for his ten-hour workday. The men wanted to work because if you did not work, you were not given food. John was still suffering from dysentery and other illnesses and recalls how one morning, after eating his one dipper-full of rotten potato soup, the food just went through him and there was no chance to break formation as they were being marched to work. It was embarrassing to be all covered in feces because there was no opportunity for him to relieve himself. He said, "There was one particular bad experience I had when a guard shoved my face in feces." There was no end to the humiliating treatment the POWs received.

What became silent revenge against their captors, the men staged their own war of sabotage at every opportunity. John said, "We were always plotting how to survive against the enemy. I was a street-wiseguy trying to steal, break, or sabotage something without being caught." John would be working on a large loom that was weaving canvass and while the guard was out of sight making his rounds, John would alter the speed of the loom, resulting in a weakened fabric. One of the machines used peanut oil and the men drained the oil and ate it. They replaced the oil with water, which would then freeze, and the machines would break down. He said, "One time I threw a spring into the transformer, which burned it out causing the power to go out. Another time, we buried a lathe in wet cement while the guards were at lunch. The poor Chinese people were getting blamed for the things we did."

While working at this textile mill, John had to meet a certain quota or else his meager food ration would be cut even more. The noise level at this mill was unbearably loud, causing the POW working next to John to jam his arm in the gears just to get out of having to work there. John went to the aid of this man, shut down the power, and tried to disengage the gears to save his friend. This act of caring on John's part lead to his own beating for trying to rescue a fellow POW.

The POWs discovered that the Chinese workers apparently had connections on the outside and were somehow able to deal goods on the black market. Capitalizing on this opportunity, the POWs devised ways to smuggle items out of the various factories and into camp. They would sneak out wire, tires, and small tools and trade with the Chinese for medicine and food.

Since the guards searched the men twice a day, as they entered and left the factories, the prisoners became adept at concealing contraband. Areas of concealment were under their armpits and in their shoes. John told of one particularly creative act of subterfuge saying, "A lot of us had problems with tapeworms and when a guy would pass a long 12-inch worm, we would save it. When we wanted to smuggle stuff into our barracks, we were supposed to get the usual 'pat down.' One guy would feign a stomach ache and another guy would display the saved worm as if the first guy just passed it from his rectum. This diversion grossed out the guards and they left us alone and we were able to smuggle our goods!"

Devising ways to stealthily deceive the opposition became a way of life. The men would steal materials they scrounged from the factories. They made their own needles to darn clothes, fashion hats from bits of cloth, and make their wooden clogs with a strap across the toes to secure them to the feet. The men had to be resourceful and used thread that was salvaged from cement bags. John was able to make himself a reversible hat of two different colors. He would cunningly wear this hat and, after a furtive glance, commit some act of stealing or sabotage. Then, he would hurriedly turn the hat inside-out, displaying a different color as part of his ruse.

Perhaps the reversible hat ploy aided in John's obtaining medicine for one of his buddies from the 31st Infantry, Company C, Ishmael Cox. Cox took a terrible beating from the guards and was nearly paralyzed from pain for weeks, thinking he was going to die. Cox later said his buddy from Lackawanna, New York, told him to hang in there. The guys couldn't get him a doctor, but they were going to find some medicine for the pain. Sure enough, a couple of days went by and the guys brought him some pills with a strict warning not to breathe a word about where the medicine came from and to take that information to the grave if he had to.

The Japanese took a perverse enjoyment in torture and beatings were a regular part of POW life. Being shorter in stature than the Americans, the Japanese would stand on boxes in order to dominate the Americans during their beatings. With a sardonic look on their faces, the Japanese unleashed their sadistic and barbaric hatred for the POWs. For no apparent reason, they would make the prisoners slap each other or have them kneel down with a 2 x 4 board under the knees.

When the men were called out for roll call, they stood in lines. A Japanese captain would then charge down the middle of the rows with his saber to straighten out the men. Any prisoner who wasn't in line would get stabbed. It seemed like the guards were always screaming and yelling in Japanese, even mistreating each other according to rank. At one point, a Japanese captain was getting punished by a colonel for something he did and had to carry a cement bag over his head. The POWs knew this would eventually trickle down the ranks and they would be punished as well. Humor certainly played a role in the POWs enduring their circumstances. John said, "Under my breath, I would mumble 'Asshole' to a guard instead of saying 'ah-so.' And there were other expletives I would utter under my breath."

A page from John's journal

While some POWs were conjuring up methods of sabotage, others were plotting how to escape from camp. Any attempt to escape, John knew, would be futile. "I was a white guy in the Orient and add to that, no one spoke English. A white guy stuck out like a sore thumb." But, desperate times sometimes call for desperate actions, as unrealistic they may be.

In April of 1943, the rumor mill was churning out information that three men were pondering an escape: Marines William Chastain and Victor Paliotti and Navy Seaman Ferdinand Merigola. It may have been POW #444 Paliotti who approached POW #433 John Zubrzycki with a request. John said, "One guy asked to trade bags with me because I had a small Filipino first aide bag and he had a larger musette bag." The rumor came to fruition and the three daring POWs escaped on June 21, 1943. The Japanese didn't discover this until the following day.

The camp whirled in a state of panic and confusion as the Japanese went ballistic. The men in the camp saw their own rations cut in half. No one was allowed near the barbed wire fence. As punishment for those who escaped, John and the others were forced to "sit" cross-legged at attention for 14 days until the three escapees were eventually found and returned to Mukden on July 6th.

It was a horrendous sight. It was obvious that the captured men had been beaten into almost oblivion, as they were semi-conscious, in a zombie-like trance, and paraded around the camp, encumbered by a steel ball and chain. Their clothing was bloody from numerous bayonet punctures. Then, they were executed in front of all the POWs, one of which was John's friend. John said, "There was a stake in the ground where the three were buried on 'Boot Hill,' with not even a cross to mark the graves. No one ever tried to escape after that." The grisly and shocking pall that hovered over the POWs was never to be forgotten. They were put into groups of 10 and if one guy escaped, the other nine would be executed.

This was enough incentive to police your buddies and keep anyone from trying to escape. John said, "You gotta realize we were like animals just trying to survive another day. As a prisoner, I felt utterly helpless. It was you and a couple of buddies against everybody else. We actually formed groups of four or five guys and we would look out for each other. Not only was it us against everybody else but you even had to keep an eye on the guys in your own group." It was a life-or-death struggle that encompassed every moment, day in and day out.

The atrocities committed by the Japanese were inconceivable as they displayed their rabid enthusiasm for torturing POWs. John was about to experience the extent the Japanese would go to in an attempt to inflict torture to the utmost. "I stole some sake with another guy because we needed something to drink due to extreme thirst. When the Japanese found out, I was interrogated and beaten severely for four days. They put me into solitary confinement, which consisted of a 4' by 4' cell for 16 days. Just to keep from going insane, I watched a spider weave its web and I killed maggots. After that, I was given an additional 14 days of punishment consisting of standing at attention from sun-up to sun-down and only one meal every third day."

This was unthinkable: John lying in a 4' by 4' cell for 16 days, curled tightly into a fetal position. His bloody body, treated like dross, was covered with bruises and swollen from repeated beatings. His mouth was like a desert of parchment from extreme thirst. His mind was numb and he no longer considered himself as a human being, but rather a tortured, ravaged animal. Survival meant separating your mind from your body in order to exist in this altered state.

No rational human would even put a dog through this type of ghastly torture. How did John maintain any semblance of sanity during this gruesome treatment? John hung tenaciously to his desire to get back home. "I had a saint for a mother. She kept me going in prison camp and I was concerned for her welfare. She was my main inspiration." Another motivator was to return home and see his school teacher, who once predicted he would wear prison stripes. He was in the crucible and pushed to the limits of the human will. "I just had *the will to survive*."

Back home Zofia, had no word about her son for almost one very long year. Time seemed to move like molasses in January. During the war, families dreaded a visit from the Western Union messenger. It meant their son was wounded – or worse. Finally, the news came one fateful day and the Zubrzyckis, holding their anxious breaths, received a telegram dated March 27, 1943, followed by a confirmation letter from the War Department as they read Sergeant John Zubrzycki was a prisoner of war. As the war dragged on, young brother Marion had enlisted in the Navy when he was 17 years old. Now, the banner displayed in Zofia's front window had two stars to signify two boys from that home were fighting for their country.

WAR DEPARTMENT

THE ADJUTANT GENERAL'S OFFICE

WASHINGTON

IN REPLY
REFER TO AG 201 Zubrzycki, John S.
(3-23-43) PC-N 032108-2

March 27, 1943.

Mr. Peter Zubrzycki,
80 Ingham Avenue,
Lackawanna, New York.

Dear Mr. Zubrzycki:

Report has been received that your son,

Sergeant John S. Zubrzycki, 6,983,553, Infantry,

is now a prisoner of war of the Japanese Government in the Philippine

Islands. This will confirm my telegram of March 27, 1943.

The Provost Marshal General, Prisoner of War Information

Bureau, Washington, D.C., will furnish you the address to which mail may

be sent. Any future correspondence in connection with his status as a

prisoner of war should be addressed to that office.

Very truly yours,

J. A. ULIO
Major General,
The Adjutant General

1 Inclosure. Memorandum re Financial Benefits.

There was no limit to the barbarism which these captured POW "animals" would be subjected. Though most of the men had no knowledge of this, some of the prisoners had become human guinea pigs, including John. Later, it was discovered that these human experiments were conducted by "Japan's diabolical Biological Warfare Unit 731."

John said, "The rumor was the doctors from Japan arrived at Mukden to see if the POWs were good for 'breeding.' They measured literally every part of our bodies. We were given unknown vials of liquids to drink as experiments and some of the guys had different reactions; some were lethal. Most of these experiments were done on the Chinese. Besides drinking this stuff, they took a feather that contained some virus and rubbed it in my nose." John recalled the doctors becoming angry that the POW test subjects were in such poor health that they were already too close to death to be viable lab specimens.

It wasn't until after the surrender of Japan that word came out about this plague research and the outcome for the doctors who committed these atrocities. In exchange for the results of their research, these despicable doctors were exonerated and let go. Decades later, the evidence of these experiments was uncovered and the truth leaked out regarding this long-kept secret. To use humans for biological experimentation was a grievous war crime.

On August 1, 1944, the War Ministry in Tokyo, Japan, issued a formal **"Kill-All Order."** The order read: *"When the battle becomes urgent the POWs will be concentrated and confined in their location and kept under heavy guard until preparations for the final disposition will be made. Although the basic aim is to act under superior orders, individual dispositions may be made in certain circumstances.* ***Whether they are destroyed individually or in groups, and whether it is accomplished by means of mass bombing, poisonous smoke, poisons, drowning, or decapitation, dispose of them as the situation dictates. It is the aim not to allow the escape of a single one, to annihilate them all, and not to leave any trace."***

It was December of 1944 and the Mukden men were looking skyward, uncertain if their eyes were deceiving them or perhaps they were hallucinating. Could it be? American bombers? The tension in the air was so thick you could cut it with a knife. It was a sight to behold— American B-29 bombers overhead!

Numerous bombs were dropped outside the compound, causing much destruction, including the munitions and railroads being blown up. However, two or three bombs were dropped right in the POW camp, killing about 19 men and injuring over 50. John said, "We were so happy and overwhelmed to see these planes, even though they bombed the camp. They were like silver jewels flying over us. The Japanese camp commander told us to write a telegram to President Roosevelt saying that we were being bombed by U.S. planes. One of our guys who lost his arm from the bombing said, 'Send the planes back. I still have one more arm.'"

Unknown to the men at the Mukden POW camp, their counterparts in a POW camp in Palawan in the Philippine Islands were to succumb to the "Kill-All-Order" on December 14, 1944. The Allied forces were advancing in the Pacific and American bombers were regularly being seen flying over the islands. During an air raid warning, the Japanese ordered the approximate 150 POWs into three covered shelter-like tunnels that were 150 feet long and four feet high. Then, the maniacal guards poured gasoline into these trenches filled with prisoners and set them on fire followed by hand grenades. Most of the screaming men were burned alive. Those who tried to run out of the trenches were shot and killed. About 30 to 40 men escaped the carnage as they climbed down or jumped over a nearby cliff and dropped down to a rocky beach area at the water's edge. As these escaping men jumped into the bay in an attempt to swim away, most were shot and killed by Japanese patrols, with only 11 men miraculously making it to safety. After swimming for hours on end in the bay, they made it to shore and ran into the jungle. They were met by Filipino guerrillas who then took them to an American camp.

When these survivors told of the horrific events at Palawan, word spread quickly that the Japanese would be annihilating all POWs as the war seemed to be nearing an end. This massacre at Palawan is what triggered the "Great Raid" by United States Army Rangers and Filipino guerrillas to make a spectacular rescue of the remaining POWs at Cabanatuan on January 30, 1945.

In August 1945, one year after it was signed, the "Kill-All Order" came precariously close to being carried out in Manchuria, China. The dire situation in Mukden was about to change as the Japanese forces were losing strength and trouble was looming on the horizon. That is, trouble for the Empire of the Rising Sun—doom for the Empire would be rising on their horizon. The pallid POWs of Mukden were down to skin and bones, mindless walking sticks, like death warmed over. Light at the end of the tunnel was a long forgotten dream. Suddenly, the light did come! Their salvation arrived in a blinding flash of light— over Hiroshima and Nagasaki.

Chapter 7

Liberation Brings Jubilation

In Lackawanna, New York, during the middle of 1945, Zofia sits on a stool as she tends to her tidy little candy store with a blank stare on her somber, lined face. Wringing her hands, she ponders the fate of her two sons who have gone off to fight the war. Frances Zubrzycki is a 22 year-old young lady now, being courted by Bernard Cerajewski (later changed to Carew). Frances has served as the family scribe, penning several letters to her brothers and sending John's letters via the Red Cross. As those years had ticked by, no word was heard from John. The last communication regarding his status was on March 27, 1943, when the War Department sent word that Sergeant Zubrzycki was a prisoner of war. Zofia's daily prayer is that John is being treated well and has ample food to eat. Her heart is heavy as she waits, her tired eyes focused on the banner with two stars that hangs in the window.

With both of her brothers gone to serve their country, Frances found work at Fishman's, the local "five and dime" store. It is here that she befriends another employee, 19 year-old Stella Antonik. Even though Stella's family lives on the "other side of the tracks," her six brothers were not exempt from going off to war. With Stella's brothers and Frances' brothers enlisted in the Armed Forces, these new friends, both from Polish families, had much in common. Much of the buzz word was about the Yanks and Allied troops making gains abroad, fueling feelings of optimism that the war might soon be over.

On the other side of the world, the men at Mukden were getting bits and pieces of rumors that the Japanese were losing the war, especially fueled by sightings of American bombers overhead and information from new POWs entering the camp. Always longing to hear word from home, little did the POWs know that there were packages and mail hidden from them for years that were stored away in the camp's warehouse. The Japanese kept the packages away from the men as another method of mental torture and evidently helped themselves to certain items after they broke open those packages.

The Red Cross only visited the camp one time. In 1945, John received just one single package over the span of three years. John said, "I got one package from home and it had already been burglarized. When I opened the package it contained a bag of peanuts and a bottle of vitamin pills." Of all the mail and packages that were sent by Frances, John only received one of those letters from home consisting of 25 words. John said, "That card partly said, 'Father is same, mother is alright, brother is in service and I got married.' That one letter I got you couldn't put a dollar amount on it. It was like lighting a candle in a dark room."

The historical moment arrived which would finally herald the end of the war. On August 6, 1945, pilot Colonel Paul W. Tibbets, Jr. closed the hatch on the American Boeing B-29 bomber named the Enola Gay. In the bay, the uranium-based-detonation atomic bomb with a code name of "Little Boy" was awaiting a date with destiny. At the appointed time and location, the bay was opened and "Little Boy" was released over Hiroshima, Japan. A blinding flash was followed by a curious mushroom cloud, reducing that city to rubble.

Just two days later, on August 8, Russia declared war on Japan. Without hesitation, on August 9, the Russians launched a massive attack into Manchuria, driving toward

Mukden. On this very same day, American lead pilot, Major Charles W. Sweeney, was flying "Bockscar" to Nagasaki, Japan. It was there that a plutonium, implosion-type atomic bomb with the code name of "Fat Man" was dropped. All was devastated and the world would never be the same.

At Mukden, there was electricity in the air with rumors spreading like wildfire. With the prisoners having no knowledge of any plan, the Office of Strategic Services (OSS), was urgently organizing a group on August 12 to save the American POWs in China due to the impending "Kill All Order" that was still in effect. The OSS was the United States wartime intelligence agency at that time and precursor to the CIA.

With the dropping of the bombs on Hiroshima and Nagasaki, Japan finally surrendered unconditionally on August 15, 1945. On that same day, at about 11:00 in the morning, several OSS men parachuted into Camp Hoten in Mukden to advise the Japanese camp commander, Colonel Matsuda, that the war was over and to order the release of the POWs. The men were shocked by all they were seeing. With craned necks as they looked skyward, their bristled hair stood on end. John said, "A team parachuted into our camp with an interpreter to prevent the execution of the POWs due to the Kill-All-Order. The Japanese were already burning their records and they were informed that the war is now over. The command was being exchanged." Leaflets were dropped, with English on one side and Japanese on the reverse, explaining the announcement of the surrender of Japanese military forces.

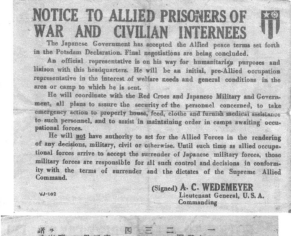

Leaflets dropped by plane into POW camp

If the OSS hadn't arrived at Mukden in time, all of the POWs would have been summarily executed. In order to carry out the Kill-All-Order, the Japanese were already preparing to march all of the POWs to the hills, followed by their execution. With the arrival of the OSS, the plans for the march came to a screeching halt. It was that close. In just days, every POW in the camp would have been eliminated.

It was on August 19 that the Russian Red Army soldiers finally arrived at Mukden. The next day was a grand day for the POWs. On August 20, the Russians disarmed the Japanese guards and their weapons were given to the POWs. The Japanese were now the prisoners of the Americans. These men will always remember August 20, 1945, as the day they were liberated by the Russians! John's heart was pounding in his chest, with eyes wider than saucers, and his palms sweaty as his liberation brought on an avalanche of suppressed emotions. What an overwhelming feeling of jubilation it was to be FREE! John said, "We were liberated by the Russians. It was a great day! It was a big day!" The impact of seeing the American flag unfurling in the breeze once again after three and one-half years was surreal. There she was, Old Glory, the beautiful red, white, and blue, as she beckoned to these brave dauntless men. Yet, despite the euphoric celebrations and realization of freedom, the first question John asked when meeting his first liberator was, "When do we eat?"

Having languished in prison camps for three and one-half years, the POWs were just a shadow of their former selves. Weighing only 89 pounds John said, "There is no way we could have survived another winter. We had been 'guests of the Emperor' for three and one-half years including surviving 'the hike,' the name we gave to the Death March." Although the Japanese surrendered on August 15, 1945, the surrender was not formally signed until September 2, aboard the battleship "USS Missouri." In the interim, planes were now flying over the camp and packages were being dropped by parachute to the skeleton-looking men below. The men were elated as they opened packages containing canned peaches, chocolate, candy, other supplies, and cigarettes. Other packages of food, clothes, and magazines were eagerly opened by the jubilant men. Much to their surprise and delight, even a movie projector and movies were air-dropped.

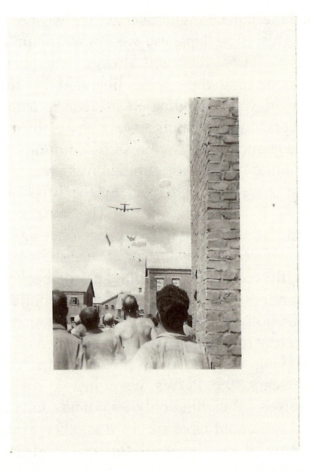

US planes making an airdrop over POWs in Mukden

Hardly believing he would be alive to witness the great day, John said, "The Japanese lined up their weapons and now we had to guard them. When a group of Russians were approaching the camp, I was at the gate of the camp and a company of scared Japanese soldiers wanted to come in for protection. Both the Russians and the Chinese were after them. A Japanese officer surrendered his sword to me. I took his saber, kicked him in the butt, and then told them to keep going and we closed the gate to them. It took a lot of restraint not to kill the Japanese. I followed orders that said there will be no retaliation against them." As a result, that group of Japanese was left to the mercy of the unforgiving Russian soldiers and Chinese. John tells of an incident involving one Japanese guard. "I reminded a guard he is supposed to commit hara-kiri (suicide by disembowelment) rather than be taken prisoner and I handed him a knife, but he refused the knife." The guard declined to fulfill his military duty to commit suicide, thus violating the centuries-old Japanese warrior Bushido Code.

and
with

John
Al

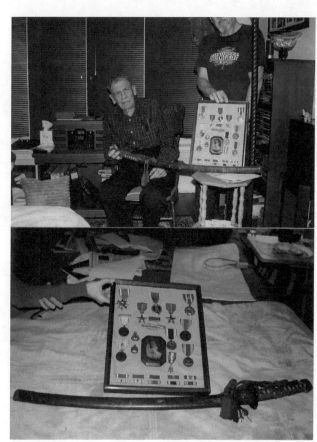

Japanese sword surrendered to John

Paper was a rare commodity and hard to come by, but John found a scrap on which he scrawled:

"8/19/45 Dear Folks, I have opportunity to write you, and not knowing how to express myself with words. The time finelly came to an end and I expect to be home in the near future. I am longing to see you people in the worst way. At the present time I am waiting for transportation. I haven't much more to say except it all seems like a dream. Your loving son, Johnny."

Four days later, he once again writes:

"Aug 23-45   Dear Folks!   I have the opportunity of sending a letter by a good friend of mine.   He is going to the states by plane and is going to a hospital.   I am writing this in a hurry, this is the best piece of paper I could get at the present moment.   Heard that we are going home by plane, last man is to be expected in two months.   I am getting back on my feet again.   I am putting on weight since we started getting food.   As I said I am writing this in a hurry, because the man is in a hurry.   Your loving Son Johnny."

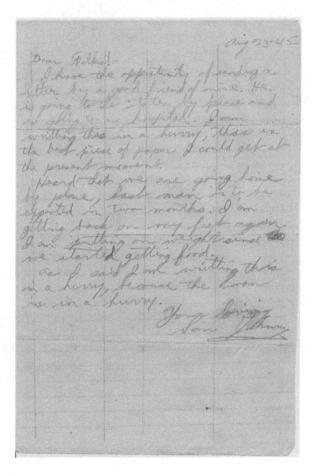

The sickest of the POWs were airlifted out of Mukden on C-47s. The railroads were still not up and running after they had been bombed. Having been liberated, the gates to the camp were open and the men could freely move about. While waiting for the railroads to be repaired, it was time to celebrate. In camp, the Russians built a stage and seating so the men could watch their Russian dancers perform. After the Russians departed, the Americans hung a large white sheet on the side of a building on which the men were able to watch movies. From the items parachuted earlier to the men, they set up the movie projector and watched Abbott and Costello, Humphrey Bogart, and cartoons. The ecstatic men were even putting on talent shows during this time of great celebration. Now devouring food with ravenous appetites, they were rapidly gaining weight and packing on the pounds.

White sheet draped on building on which movies were
shown to the liberated POWs

The pass reads, *"HEADQUARTERS, CAMP HOTEN, MUKDEN, MANCHURIA PERMANENT PASS August 26, 1945 The Bearer, Sgt. Zubrzycki, John S. Whose signature appears below is authorized to leave camp and visit Mukden and vicinity from 7:30 AM to 7:00 PM daily. By command of Major General PARKER. (Signed by E.T. HALSTEAD, Lieutenant Colonel, A.G.D. Adjutant General) (Signed by John S. Zubrzycki)*

Anxious to get out of camp and "paint the town red," the men were issued passes to go into downtown Mukden, where they proceeded to drink and look for women. In John's recount of these excursions, he said, "Food, cigarettes, and coffee is what we wanted the most. We could not go home until they repaired the damaged railroad and it would be many weeks or months. We went to town and were getting drunk with the Russian liberators. We even held up a bank and gave the loot away like it was confetti to the Chinese while we rode around on top of Russian trucks, just throwing the money away. We stole some beer. The Russians were brutal."

A photo John carried in his wallet until the day he passed away was of a young Russian soldier who wrote in Russian on the reverse of the photo, "For memory keepsakes, to the American on the day of his liberation from the Japanese camp – Ivan Olkachev, 3-9-45" (September 3, 1945).

Mukden City

Mukden City

WASHINGTON DC SEPT 10 401P

HOME SERVICE, AMERICAN RED CROSS

SGT JOHN S ZUBRZYCKI 6983553 REQUESTS PETER ZUBRZYCKI

16 CLARK STREET LACKAWANNA BE NOTIFIED HIS LIBERATION

SENDS BEST WISHES HOPES TO BE HOME SOON.

NATIONAL HEADQUARTERS

AMERICAN RED CROSS

LA9 GOVT DL PD WASHINGTON DC 1005P OCT 21

PETER ZUBRZYCKI

80 INGHAM AVE LACKA NY

THE SECRETARY OF WAS HAS ASKED ME TO INFORM YOU THAT YOUR SON SGT

ZUBRZYCKI JOHN S HAS BEEN RETURNED TO MILITARY CONTROL 20 SEPT 45 HE

WAS EVACUATED TO UNITED STATES ON 1 OCTOBER AND IS DUE TO ARRIVE AT SAN

FRANCISCO CALIFORNIA ON 21 OCTOBER PERIOD HE WILL BE GIVEN AN OPPORTUNITY

TO COMMUNICATE WITH YOU UPON ARRIVAL. THIS ARRIVAL INFORMATION IS TENTATIVE

AT THIS TIME AND IS SUBJECT TO CHANGE IF SUCH CHANGE IS NECESSARY TO MEET

MILITARY REQUIREMENTS PERIOD EVERY EFFORT WILL BE MADE TO INFORM YOU IF

CHANGES ARE MADE IN SCHEDULE OR ARRIVAL PORT

EDWARD F WITSELL ACTING THE ADJUTANT GENERAL OF THE ARMY

918A

Finally, the day came to leave and begin the homeward journey. The remainder of the men departed Mukden on September 11, 1945. As John sat in the truck pulling out of the camp, he turned for a long last look. Clutching the Japanese saber, with dust churning up from the road, his view eventually became obscured as the camp became a dot in the distance. There was also a distance that had been placed between his humanity and reality. In his mind, he realized he had lost his youth and had been living like an animal for so many years. He became hardened by all the death and horrors that surrounded him for so long and it changed him forever. What will it be like to be home again? Lost in his thoughts, the truck ride heading southwest for several hours slowed to a stop.

For the next leg of the journey home, the men jumped off the truck and boarded a train that would take them to the southern end of the Liaoning Province of China. After a full day of travel, the men arrived at the commercial port of Dairen (situated near the Yellow Sea), which has year-round access to the Pacific Ocean. Dairen is also known as Dalian and Port Arthur.

In Dairen, the men boarded the hospital ship, the "USS Relief," on September 13 to begin the voyage to Okinawa. Life for these forgotten souls certainly "took a 180." Here, they were chowing down scrumptious food like there was no tomorrow, being fully aware that there almost was "no tomorrow" for them. They were given 24-hour access to the mess hall/galley. They savored the flavors as they sunk their teeth into tender juicy steaks along with mountains of steaming hot mashed potatoes overflowing with luscious gravy. The aromas were dizzying. After a much needed and welcomed bath, they were given new clothes and enjoyed sleeping on real beds with clean sheets and a pillow! Freedom never felt so good.

John wrote home and most likely intended the date to be September 15, not August 15, 1945:

"*Dear Folks: --*

Writting you a few lines letting you know where I'm at and how I feel. Since I've been freed and eating all the food I can hold you would never recognize me. I probably will weigh about 170 lbs. when I get home.

We left (Mukden) for (Dairen) and went aboard a Red Cross ship called the (Relief) and sailed to (Okinawa).

I'm writing this letter from the ship which is anchored at Okinawa.

My health has improved a 100%. I hope everybody at home is still in good health. Haven't much more to say. Incidentally I'm writting this letter in bed, I'm ready to go to sleep.

Your loving son

Johnny

P.S. Give my regards to the boys and.....I hope you can read this scribbling.

Aug 15, 1945

Dear Folks:—

Writing you a few lines letting you know where I'm at and how I feel. Since I've been freed and eating all the food I can hold, you wouldn't hardly recognize me. I probably will weigh about 176 lbs. when I get home.

We left (Mukden) for (Dairen) and went aboard a Red Cross ship called the (Relief) and sailed to (Okinawa).

I'm writing this letter from the ship which is anchored at Okinawa.

My health has improved a 100%. I hope everybody at home is still in good health. There isn't much more to say. Incidentally I'm writing this letter in bed, I'm ready to go to sleep.

your loving son

Johnny

P.S. Give my regards to the boys and

(I hope you can read this scribbling.)

As their "luck" would have it, they were not yet out of the woods as more obstacles kept blocking their path. The Japanese had planted floating mines in the water and the men were told to be on the lookout for them. When a mine was sighted, it was fired upon and exploded. One other ship did take a hit from one of these floating mines, but all the men aboard were spared.

Mother Nature also threw a kink into the trip by unleashing a vicious typhoon, which was heading toward their destination of Okinawa. They had to pull up anchor and ride out the storm in the open sea. The towering waves made the ship bounce up and down like a bobber on a fishing line, tossing the men about. As the storm subsided, the railings of the ship were all bent out of shape as the men surveyed the damage. Coincidentally, John's brother, Marion, was on sea duty with the Navy and only later learned that he was in close proximity of John. Had the brothers known of each other's location, they may have reunited had it not been for this unfortunate typhoon.

In Okinawa John received the routine briefing and medical treatment before boarding a plane that would take him to Manila. Having not lost his sense of humor and eagerness to leave his mark, he scrawled on an outhouse wall, "Kilroy was here." Soon, he will have gone full circle from where this unbelievable experience started in the Philippine Islands in what seemed eons ago. Fate must have been on the side of this boy from Lackawanna who was like "the cat with nine lives." As he was being flown to the Philippine Islands, the plane that was to land before his had crashed and the runway had to be cleared before John's plane could land. Fate was on his side once again. What are the odds of defying death under so many circumstances for so many years? On September 27, 1945, he earned the curved stripe referred to as "a rocker," as he was promoted to Staff Sergeant.

The final leg home had John boarding a ship in Manila for San Francisco, California, departing the Pearl of the Orient forever. Now, on October 20, 1945, over one month from having departed Mukden, John's odyssey had miraculously come to an end. There is no victory without conflict. On that day, when John arrived in California, perhaps for a brief moment he felt like a victor. After the ship docked, his hand clutched the railing as he steadied himself while descending the gangplank. Thoughts flooded his mind after having lived a lifetime in those three and one-half years when his freedom was stripped away.

His knees were shaking as he set foot on US soil. He stopped, knelt down, and kissed the ground. John later said, "My prison life was too much of everything. If you lost your will, you died." He was a survivor and the common thread that was woven through these men was *the will to survive*.

Chapter 8

Home Sweet Home

Rising from his knees as though on holy ground, Sergeant Zubrzycki collected himself and took in the smells and sounds of the bay, reminding himself he is still property of the United States government. The now former POWs were ushered off to Letterman General Hospital in San Francisco, California, for further tests and medical evaluation before their departure to various hometowns across the country.

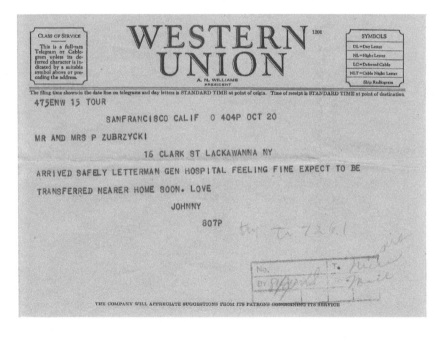

As part of their debriefing, they had a meeting with a Military Intelligence officer. John said, "Our debriefer was a major in Military Intelligence and he asked us to raise our right hands. We were instructed to swear to never divulge any of the details of our captivity. Seeing as how we were still in the Army and the officer was from Army MI, we reacted as if we were sworn under orders to obey until further notice." They were all going home but weren't permitted to talk about what they went through! A fellow Mukden survivor, James Bollich, wrote about his experience in "A Soldier's Journal." Bollich stated, "One thing I never talked about while in college was my experience in the service. I was still abiding by the military's request not to tell about your POW experience to anyone."

When they returned home, many of the POWs came to realize their nerves were shot and they were jittery and shaking. Many didn't talk about their prison experiences because they said, "Nobody would believe it." John would later lament that he still couldn't believe he went through this, and that it seemed like a bad dream. Having been duly instructed not to discuss their experiences with anyone, the ex-POWs did not "throw a pity party" for themselves because they were expected to suck it up and get over it.

World War II left millions dead across the world. Estimated United States military deaths were approximately 405,399.[3] Those soldiers never made it back home. An estimated 20 million military and civilian Chinese and 20 million military and civilian Soviets were lost during the war. The cost of war was not just monetary. The psychological impact on the human mind is what was even more costly. The POWs were scarred for life. Their lives had been ravaged and their youth stripped away. After the war, they tried to block out the memories. The war was not over for them, and it still raged in their minds, reliving it through nightmares and with bodies racked with pain.

---

[3] From the "World Book Encyclopedia," Alice M. Verbeme, Gannett News Service

Taking a long drag on his cigarette, John contemplated his future as he gazed across the hospital room. Still unable to grasp the actualization of total freedom, he was feeling like a stranger in his own skin. He endured and survived events of cataclysmic magnitude that defy belief. As he exhaled the smoke from his lungs forming rings in the air, he dared not close his eyes for fear of waking from this dream and plunging back into the hell from which he just emerged. The nightmares surely came with a vengeance later.

It was time to board the train that would take him to Utica, New York. Six days after arriving in the States, on October 26, 1945, the 23-year-old soldier arrived at Rhodes General Hospital. After 15 days of medical treatment and recuperation, John wrote home on November 10. The letter reads:

Hello Folks: --
Just writing a few lines letting you know I got here safely. They took an Xray today and so far they can't locate my medical records you know the stuff they took when I left here, such as bloodcounts & the rest of the check up so I guess I'll have to take them over again.
I've started eating again & my nerves are getting settled.
I can't get over the way everybody has been treating me, I could swear to Christ it was just to good to last as long as it did. I probably didn't show my appreciation like I should of, but I didn't know how to express my feelings.
Give my regards to the family.
Yours, Johnny
(over) Tell Mr. and Mrs. Grzybowski that Turkey isn't here as yet."

11/19/45

Hello Folks:—

Just writing a few lines letting you know I got here safely. They took an x ray today and so far they can't locate my medical records you know the stuff they took when I left here, such as blood counts & the rest of the check up so I guess I'll have to take them over again.

I've started eating again my nerves are getting settled.

I can't get over the way everybody has been treating me, I could swear to Christ it was just to good to last as long as it did. I probably didn't show my appreciation like I should of, but I didn't know how to express my feelings.

Give my regards to the family.

Yours
Johnny

(OVER)

Tell Mr. & Mrs. Szyglowski that turkey isn't here as yet.

Then came the time he both welcomed, yet dreaded, when he was given a pass to go home for 90 days of R & R. What was the likelihood of having any semblance of returning to a "normal" life? Trying to steady a cup of coffee in his hand he became painfully aware that his hands were shaking and he was sweating profusely. John said, "I didn't want to go home right away because I couldn't face it."

JOHN S. ZUBRZYCKI

To you who answered the call of your country and served in its Armed Forces to bring about the total defeat of the enemy, I extend the heartfelt thanks of a grateful Nation. As one of the Nation's finest, you undertook the most severe task one can be called upon to perform. Because you demonstrated the fortitude, resourcefulness and calm judgment necessary to carry out that task, we now look to you for leadership and example in further exalting our country in peace.

Harry Truman

THE WHITE HOUSE

Early in December, John found himself in his hometown of Lackawanna, NY, standing in front of 16 Clark Street in his pressed Army uniform. He stopped in his tracks in front of his parents' house and paused, taking it all in. After a moment's hesitation, he walked up the front steps to the door, turned the door handle, and stepped inside. Upon seeing her son for the first time in over five years, Zofia gasped and said, "Mój synek, Jashu" (Polish for "My son, Johnny"). Her eyes then rolled back in their sockets, her face was ashen from shock, and she passed out! The emotional impact was overwhelming and, when she finally regained consciousness, the tears of happiness flowed like a joyful river.

Frances, John, and Zofia

During the years of the war, not much had changed in Lackawanna. The plant still spewed plumes of soot from the tall smoke stacks with the daily grind of life going on as usual. But the years of the war *did* change John profoundly. He was a different man, as he secretly dealt with the deeply-rooted effects of war and was in the throes of adapting to a civilization he had left behind in his youth.

While away from home, John was always worried that his mother was taking beatings and he wasn't there to protect her. Thoughts of her sustained him during those dark, bleak years. Growing up with an abusive father, John never stood up to him and received his share of unwarranted beatings.

One day, while at home with his folks, the day of reckoning came for Piotr. Piotr started his usual rant, raised his fists, and started to beat the meek Zofia. In an instant, John sprung to his feet like a lion leaping on its prey and yanked Piotr off of his mother. John had the specter of death in his eyes as he grabbed his father and sternly warned, "No more beatings, Pa. No more. Don't you ever lay a hand on Ma again." That threatening look of hellfire raging in John's eyes was enough to put the fear of God in Piotr's heart as he trembled. From that moment forward, Piotr never laid a finger on Zofia.

A few weeks later, with Johnny safely home, family and friends wished to celebrate his return from the war and captivity. It was party time! "Welcome home, Johnny!!" John's cousins, Pearl and Joanie Duma, invited around 30 guests to a bash. The party was held at Joanie's beauty shop, where sketches of hair-dos adorned the walls. Tables were set up and covered with white tablecloths. Then came the scrumptious food. Smacznego!! That is, "tasty and delicious" in Polish. Platters filled the tables with *pierogi* (filled dumplings), *gołabki* (stuffed cabbage rolls), *kapustą and kielbasa* (sauerkraut with sausage), and *placek* (coffee cake). A toast was given as glasses filled with *Krupnik* (spiced Vodka) were raised high; belting out the lyrics from the traditional Polish toast, "Sto lat, sto lat, niech żyje, żyje nam" (may you live a hundred years). The booze was flowing and spirits ran high. Cousin Pearl's infectious laugh could be heard in the crowd as she was throwing back her head in laughter, while cousin Joanie, with her polio, could be seen limping about in her "beauty shop-turned party place." Colored streamers were gaily draped on the revelers shoulders.

Bottom photo: Arrow indicates John with Stella behind him and Zofia to the right of John

John's sister, Frances, was up to playing match-maker for her older brother. Their brother, Marion, was still serving in the Navy overseas. She conveniently arranged for her co-worker, Stella Antonik, to be in attendance at this party. At 19 years of age, Stella was a comely young lady and was quick to turn the head of Johnny. She was stunning in her floral dress, her brunette hair in a striking up-do, and lips covered in a bright red lipstick. She had a sparkle in her eye and a heart of gold. That was the moment the two of them "hit it off," and the rest is history.

One disheartening situation for Johnny came later that evening. As he sunk down in the soft cushions of a sofa, the air was thick with a lingering haze of cigarette smoke, and ashtrays were filled with snuffed-out butts. One of the guests had a map of the world and located the Philippine Islands. Pointing to the islands, a female guest laughingly mocked as to what the big deal was about being captured during the war. She ignorantly said, "Look how close you were to the mainland being only an inch away. Why didn't you just swim across the water?" John knew at that moment that nobody could even begin to know what he had just endured and that they were completely clueless. He growled to himself in Polish, "Głupi stara baba" (stupid old lady), as the party wound down. The merriment subsided and the tipsy revelers departed.

Now alone in the darkness of his room, John sits quietly, staring at the glowing ember on his cigarette. He takes a long drag, flicks off the ash, and snuffs out the butt. Nighttime brought with it the nightmares that would haunt him for the rest of his life. While trying to calm his mind in order to get some much-needed sleep, his vivid thoughts robbed him of any peace as they transported him back to being a captive POW.

Years of deprivation, cruelty, and trying to just live through another day lent adjusting to a social life seemingly impossible. Coming back home meant a different kind of struggle to survive, and turning to alcohol and withdrawing seemed to offer a way out for many of the former prisoners of war. Happiness was elusive.

Upon returning home, he said, "I had a hard time becoming a civilian. I had dog tags from deceased POWs that I returned to the families. I was concerned about opening wounds when I returned the dog tags, but also recognized that with this contact, the door was closed and helpful to these families." He recalled an incident when he travelled to a fallen G.I.'s home to return the soldier's dog tags to his parents. "Why did YOU get to come back when my son didn't," asked the distraught mother. John felt the mother's grief and the burden of his task. "I didn't want to do much more of that anymore," he remembered.

At the age of 24, on March 22, 1946, Staff Sergeant John Zubrzycki was Honorably Discharged at Fort McPherson, Georgia. Upon being "separated" from the regular Army, he enlisted in the Army Reserves that same day. It was time to try to put the broken pieces of his life back together.

Back in Lackawanna, John was on the right track to living a normal life, having met Stella at his homecoming party. Well, maybe it wasn't the right "track," since Stella had been instructed earlier not to date boys from the "other side of the tracks!" Stella was smitten by John's blue eyes and his "tough guy" demeanor. Knowing that her parents would not approve of her dating someone from the other side of the tracks, her brothers would sneak her out of her bedroom window so she could meet up with her Johnny. John's brother, who had just come home from the Navy, said that John's feet would hurt so badly from the war that he would walk home barefoot, carrying his shoes, after seeing Stella.

John needed to find employment and jobs were hard to come by after the war. He did get a job through veterans services with a company where retail store window display shelving was made. It didn't work out. John hated being "cooped up" indoors, where employees were not allowed to smoke. He was not in a good state of mind. Instructions from supervisors reminded him of orders from prison guards. He finally walked off the job, lighting a cigarette before leaving. Eventually, in November 1946, he found work at the Bethlehem Steel Plant in Lackawanna, all the while he was courting Stella.

Top: Stella
Bottom left: John and Stella
Bottom right: Marion and John

Poet Robert Frost said in *The Road Not Taken*, "Yet knowing how way leads on to way," so it was with John and Stella. After a year of dating, they were married on Tuesday, January 21, 1947, at Saint Barbara's Catholic Church in Lackawanna. They made their home on Clark Street before moving to Wasson Avenue. Here was John, miraculously back home in his old neighborhood, with all kinds of emotions swirling through his mind. This just might be the start to living a normal life again.

Stella hanging laundry in Lackawanna, NY

Before the Korean War broke out, at the age of 27, John was Honorably Discharged from the Army Reserves, on March 21, 1949. He and Stella were starting a family and the idea of moving to where the air was fresher and the yards were bigger for children to play was appealing. They packed up and moved a few suburbs southeast of Lackawanna to Hillside Avenue in Orchard Park in June 1950.

Then came the babies. Their firstborn was a boy, Allen, who was born in August 1950. It was at this time that John wanted to legally change their last name. This was a difficult decision, so he sought Zofia's advice. "Why not?," she asked. "If women can do it, why not a man?" On September 12, 1950, the surname was changed from Zubrzycki to Zale. Of course Allen should have a little sister, so in October 1952, Karen was born. Unbeknownst to Karen, in over 60 years hence, she would be writing this story.

The newly minted John Zale was still having difficulties adjusting to the protocols of civilian life. When he went to the Roman Catholic priest at his family's church to arrange a christening for baby Allen, he was rebuffed. The priest challenged that John wasn't tithing enough and compared him to the donations of a local restaurant owner. There was an argument and John ended up taking his son to another relative's church, Our Lady of the Sacred Heart, to arrange the Rite of Baptism. Finally, the young father angrily took his family out of the Catholic Church. That move earned him the scorn of some devout Catholic family members, as nearly all Poles and Polish immigrants were. Leaving the church was unthinkable! The Zale family subsequently joined the Wesleyan Church of Orchard Park.

The daily grind of life churned on. After nine years of working dangerous jobs at Bethlehem Steel, John left the plant on October 15, 1955. His departure came after an incident at the plant, where an executive learned of John's wartime travails and wanted to personally hear his story. At the same time, he was having even more difficulties sleeping when he was put on the midnight shift. His shop steward said John could get off of working midnights if he would wash the steward's car and speak to the curious executive. The young employee grabbed a bucket and sponge, went out to the car, and promptly urinated on the front tire and fender. His career at Bethlehem Steel promptly ended! Some time later, he found employment working as a carpenter for the Navy Reserve Center located in Niagara Falls, NY. Since this was prior to a section of the New York State Thruway highway system being built, the daily commute from Orchard Park to Niagara Falls on secondary roads was long, aggravating, and very much less than desirable.

John and Stella went house hunting just south of the Niagara Falls area. Circa 1957 "B.M." ("Before McDonalds" in Western New York), the family of four was packed up and, with their young children in tow, moved to Spaulding Street in North Tonawanda. Stella and John lived at this home for the remainder of their lives.

John arrived at a "kairos" moment in his life. Merriam-Webster defines this word of Greek origin as, "a time when conditions are right for the accomplishment of a crucial action: the opportune and decisive moment."

The capacity to control one's destiny is in each one of us. It is in embryo just waiting to be born. For John, it was a propitious moment for decision and action. The years of trauma became the wellspring to greatness.

* * *

"The world breaks everyone and afterward many are strong in the broken places. But those that will not break it kills. It kills the very good and the very gentle and the very brave impartially. If you are none of these you can be sure it will kill you too but there will be no special hurry." -- From "A Farewell to Arms" by Ernest Hemingway

Chapter 9

Jump Abie

A businessman wants to teach his young son, Abie, how to be successful. At the small store, there are shelves upon shelves of merchandise, some of which can only be reached by ladder.

One day, the father asks Abie to go up a few steps on the ladder, with which Abie complies. The father says, "Son, I want you to jump from the ladder and I will catch you." The boy turns to look over his shoulder and says, "Papa, I'm afraid! What if you don't catch me?" The father says assuredly, "Trust me, I'm your father. Jump, Abie." A bit shaken and nervous, the boy jumps into the arms of his father.

"Now go back on the ladder and go up a few rungs higher this time," the father instructs. Abie climbs the ladder a few extra steps and again his father says, "Jump, son." "Papa I'm too scared!" "Trust me, I'm your father. Jump, Abie, and I will catch you." Reluctantly, Abie jumps and safely lands in the loving arms of his father.

"This time, I want you to go to the top of the ladder," the father commands. Abie complies, now having gained some confidence. "Jump, Abie." Precariously perched at the top of the shaking ladder, the lad gets a sudden lump in his throat and cries, "Papa how do I know you will catch me?" "Trust me, I'm your father. Now jump, Abie."

Abie jumps and the father steps aside as his young son crashes to the floor. "Abie, you just learned a lesson in life: Don't trust anyone, not even your father."

Now it is my turn to continue the story about the enigmatic John S. Zubrzycki, aka John Zale, aka Dad. This story about Abie and his father is one that Dad told repeatedly to me (his daughter, Karen) and to Al (his son, Allen). There were dozens of other "Dad-isms" such as, "If you want to dance, you have to pay the band." Another favorite was, "When you point your finger accusingly at someone, be aware that your three other fingers are pointing directly back at you." These tidbits were his way of sharing his lessons on life; wisdom seen through his eyes.

I sat down at the computer, gazed up and stared at the ceiling, searching my thoughts. It was time to take a trip into the distant past and relive those years of growing up with Dad, knowing very little about his war experience back then. The hot steam was rising from a cup of steeping tea, as my eyes followed the skinny string from the tea bag to the little white tag at the other end. Interestingly, the tag had a quote from Ralph Waldo Emerson, "The creation of a thousand forests is in one acorn." In hindsight, I now understand how Dad dealt with his traumatized past by choosing to make a difference in the life of others. Whether by design or chance, he committed himself to be a positive influence, as he lived by good example and actually "walked the talk."

There is something to be said about family dynamics where there are members living with a former prisoner of war. Mom, Al, and I were all clueless about the inordinate and debilitating trauma Dad experienced over so many years. Why? Because he was ordered by the Army not to talk about it! Yet the importance of sharing those atrocities through compassionate and healing discussion was the very thing he was prohibited to do.

Not having much (if any) knowledge of the Pacific Theater, it did not interest us to research the topic on our own. For my generation, this was a time before personal computers and search engines, such as Google. All I knew was that a web site was a misspelling for where a creepy spider lived. To do research for homework assignments, we would trot down to the local public library and flip through the drawers of index cards in the Dewey Decimal System. After laboriously locating books on the shelves, it was a matter of flipping through pages of musty smelling tomes or going through volumes of hard-covered encyclopedias.

Among the piles of papers and books found in Dad's bedroom after he passed away, was a textbook, "*The Story of World War II*," by Robert Leckie, Copyright 1964. This is a textbook, specifically on World War II, mind you. The book is one-inch thick and contains 192 pages. While the book has extensive information about the bombing of Pearl Harbor, it has only two pages about the Japanese airstrikes that were happening simultaneously in the Pacific (Philippine Islands, Guam, and others). Later, there is only one paragraph about the liberation of American prisoners of war, including three words, "the Death March," with no further details. There was no mention of the atrocities at Cabanatuan, the Hell Ships, or the Mukden, Manchuria, POW camp.

What about the daily struggles of the captured prisoners, abandoned by their government, who were trying to stay alive another day? It isn't any wonder why the spouses and children of POWs were totally unaware of the internal strife of their loved one. As stated, Dad never talked about it. As it turns out, what the war veterans experienced was far outside the scope of what the average person could even begin to comprehend.

Interestingly, in World War II there was no labeling for Post-Traumatic Stress Disorder, or PTSD. Back in those days, it was referred to as "battle fatigue." Soldiers with combat exhaustion were expected to return to combat after given some rest. It wasn't until 35 years after Dad was liberated that the American Psychiatric Association added PTSD to the "Diagnostic and Statistical Manual of Mental Disorders" in 1980. By this time, Dad was already 58 years old.

For the former prisoners of war, the world just moved on. Time passed, and they had been all but forgotten. Outwardly, Dad wore a mask of well being, while inwardly he roiled from an array of deep-rooted vexations. The demons he had to fight in his mind never left him. However, he was able to find strength and purpose in controlling those demons.

This became his kairos moment of decision. With a wife and two young children, he committed himself to self-sacrificing service for his family, his fellow patriots, and the community. He willed himself to transcend his afflictions and found his true passion. Daniel Goleman says in "*Emotional Intelligence*" (New York: Bantam Book, 1995), "A life without passion would be a dull wasteland of neutrality, cut off and isolated from the richness of life itself." Dad's **will to survive** and his passion for life was the fuel that enriched the lives of so many people that he touched. He was extremely humble. He got outside of himself and found a greater cause.

For starters, I have to emphasize that our mother, Stella, was a SAINT! She stuck it out with my dad until her passing from breast cancer when she was 69 years old. It is an understatement to say she was the glue that held our family together. She was the anchor for my dad and us kids.

When you are a just a kid growing up, you have no yardstick to measure what is normal and what is just plain weird. Besides Boy Scouts, Girl Scouts, and school activities, we pretty much just lived a reclusive life style. We had a negligible social life, and there were never any

125

parties at our home. Not once, ever, did my parents hire a baby sitter and "go out." If an event didn't include the whole family, we stayed home. We never, ever went out to dinner to a restaurant until Al was 18 years old and was graduating from high school. Imagine that! Not going out to dinner for 18 years, other than going on occasion to visit our grandparents or to eat at the homes of relatives.

At the dinner table at home, Dad would sit in a modified cross-legged position on the chair, almost like a half-squat, half crouch. Mom would say something to him in Polish and he would put his legs down and sit normal on the chair. (Back in the days as a prisoner of war, this is how the men sat on the ground.)

Sometimes, Dad would get in an agitated state and Al and I would scatter, while Mom walked around "on eggshells." He never slept well at night. That is when the demons would enter his mind and he wrestled with the devil. In the morning, his sheets and blanket would be all wrapped up in one big knot in the middle of the bed. Eventually, Mom and Dad slept in separate twin beds (as I later learned), because he would get so violent tossing and turning from horrific nightmares that both of them feared for her safety. He never was able to talk about it and explain his behavior. Mom would wonder what it was that she did wrong that caused him to act this way.

Having suffered from malnutrition during the war, and a result of having had beriberi, his feet burned all the time for years after the war. His suffering manifested itself in many ways. He was a tough guy, and being very stubborn, he would never let anyone help or assist him, insisting on personal independence.

Nonetheless, Mom filled our home with love and carried on unselfishly and courageously caring for her family. Dad was a wonderful father in that he wanted his children to have a better life than what was dealt to him, and he worked very hard to provide for us. He made sure we were exposed to as many different and interesting opportunities as possible. Boy Scouts and Girl Scouts were a huge part of our family life. Our parents also got us involved with camping, canoeing, downhill skiing, nature studies, survival skills, swimming, playing musical instruments, and so much more. Doing well in school was paramount and getting an education was stressed. I could not have asked for better parents. They both loved their family deeply and were self-sacrificing. Family always came first.

Al, Karen, and Dad canoeing in the "Tamarack"

To foster our spiritual enrichment, every Sunday found us worshiping at the Nash Road Free Methodist Church in North Tonawanda, New York. Dad would be belting out in a loud baritone voice, "O Lord my God.

When I in awesome wonder, consider all the worlds Thy hands have made, I see the stars, I hear the rolling thunder, Thy power throughout the universe displayed. Then sings my soul, my Savior God to Thee: How great Thou art, how great Thou art." There was thunder in his voice and I imagine the church rafters shook. Our folks made sure we attended Sunday school and placed a Bible in our hands. Those were some happier times among the darker moments for Dad.

Who was to know that Dad's vivid painful memories were an insidious cancer eating away at him and robbing him of peace of mind. He did some pretty strange stuff that were reflections of his prisoner experience, but I didn't know otherwise since I was just a young kid. Why would he drill a three-foot by three-foot hole through the cement wall in the basement that led to a small space under the house and then fill it with shelves, canned goods, and an air vent? For fun, I would crawl inside, shut the little wooden door, and turn on the electric light and fan. Dad also drilled a hole in our living room ceiling, where he constructed a metal chimney and installed a pot-bellied stove.

In our backyard was a really fancy brick fireplace, which was about 12 feet long and had two tiers on either side of the tall chimney. The original owners had it built for outdoor party-type grilling. We kids would climb all over it and jump off of it, playing imaginary games. For reasons unknown, Dad took a sledgehammer to it and dismantled it brick by brick. He detached the courtesy lights in the car so it would be pitch dark when you opened the door. Then there was the time he took spray paint and covered the glass windows on the garage door so no one could peer inside. He was mysterious and clandestine in his behavior. He was an enigma.

Having only had a sixth-grade education, Dad became self-schooled. He craved knowledge and had a voracious appetite for reading. It seemed as though he would read anything he could get his hands on that pertained to do-it-yourself projects or science and nature. Regularly, he would visit the North Tonawanda Library and check out the maximum number of books allowed. Piles and piles of books always surrounded his chair in the living room. Stopping at yard sales, he would bring home boxes of books, saying that if he learns just one thing from that box of books, it was worth it.

A noteworthy part of Dad's mentality was what he called "bartering." He would try to hoard everything in the event of a war or a breakdown in social order. When I asked him why he kept all this "junk," he would say that someday we might need what I called junk to barter for food. We might need to barter some tools for food or water. Amazingly, Mom was able to keep his hoarding to a minimum and actually maintained a clean, tidy and cozy home.

But, to fast-forward momentarily, the hoarding all changed after Mom passed away. It got so bad with the mountains of stuff he collected, that you could barely make your way through the bedroom. Forget trying to navigate the narrow path through the garage or basement. In my adult years when I would travel on vacation from my home in Vermont to stay at Dad's house, I would have to sleep with my suitcase on the bed because there was no room on the floor to place it due to all his piles of "treasures."

After Dad passed away, my husband, Kerry, and I filled 10 construction-sized dumpsters with moldy junk, in addition to four-and-a half truckloads of items taken to auction. That is in addition to all the items that friends took and truckloads of books for the library and clothes to the

Good Will. What was really amazing was the amount of hazardous materials he had stashed away, "just in case." We made several trips to the hazardous waste disposal location to get rid of liquid mercury that weighed three pounds, Dinitrophenylhydrazine, large bottles of chloroform and ammonia, countless spray cans, and several unmarked, unidentifiable liquids. The poverty of childhood and life-threatening deprivation of prison camp made telling and lasting impacts on our father.

Before and after photos of basement. Arrows indicate glass counter

Top photo: Bedroom; Bottom photo Kerry in garage

Now, getting back to growing up with Dad, he introduced the family to tent camping early on. I was only four years old when we went on our first camping trip. Camping was pretty rugged back in 1956, and Dad and Al would pitch a canvas tent, while Mom set up a makeshift "kitchen" on a picnic table under a tarp. I don't recall seeing any mobile-type campers back in those days. We would gather small branches and lash them together to make a small table or a tripod to hold a washbasin. On one camping trip, Al accidentally slipped with a hatchet while chopping wood and seriously cut his hand. Mom got nauseous at the sight of the bloody gash. Calmly, Dad got out his first-aid kit and skillfully butterfly-stitched Al's hand, treated it with some sort of disinfectant, and bandaged it in sterile gauze. That was it. No hospital, no doctor, just Dad doing his survival thing.

Eight-year old Karen during family camping trip

Zale family on camping outings

After about seven years of family camping trips during summer vacation, Dad didn't like the idea that the state campgrounds were getting too crowded with other folks, and the price for a campsite soared to the exorbitant price of around two dollars a night. It was time to buy a little piece of paradise in the country that Dad could call his own. In 1963, when I was 11 years old and Al was 13, this dream came to fruition. Mom and Dad purchased 101 acres of land in Mansfield, New York, about an hour and a half drive south from the city. The nearby, now-booming vacation destination of Holiday Valley in nearby Ellicottville didn't even exist back then.

From here on out, our family time on weekends was spent at this seemingly vast piece of woodland in the middle of nowhere. There was no electricity and no running water, just acres of woods. No one lived on our country dirt road, which was closed during the winter snow season. We were very secluded there. After countless times of pitching a tent and "roughing it" out in the wilderness, Dad had an idea. He decided to erect a shelter, similar to those found in the state and county parks. Since the wind seemed to usually blow from one direction, after some time, Mom suggested he build a wall on that side to cut down on stuff blowing all around under the shelter. Once that was done, it seemed the wind came from a different side, so another wall went up. Before long, Dad enclosed the whole shelter with walls and lots of windows on all sides, plus a door.

Even though this was our place to escape to and "get away from it all," Dad was driven to work hard to the point of fatigue and exhaustion. We didn't realize this was his way of not thinking about the past horrors that plagued him. He cherished his freedom and would say, "If I want to chop down that tree, I will. And if I want to plant a tree there, I can do that, too!" Mom would try to convince him to sit down and relax. He was like the Energizer Bunny seen in the commercials, who keeps beating on the drum, non-stop. Dad just kept going and going and going like that bunny. He was never able to rest.

Over time, Dad had built a cabin out of that shelter pretty much all by himself with scrap and salvaged materials. We did help on one family project, where Al and Dad wheeled in heavy loads of dirt and stones on top of the existing grass and then built a wooden floor for the "shack," as he called it. The roof was made of heavy-gauge corrugated steel, difficult to hoist in place and affix to the rafters. Later, Dad said he wanted Al to see how difficult physical labor can be. This was a lesson that we should study and do well in school, learning to use our brains and not our backs. "If you don't have it up here," he would say (pointing to his head), "you'd better have it back here," (pointing to his lower back).

Al working at the cabin

The family cabin in Mansfield, NY

Dad even built an extension on the back, put in a homemade wood-burning stove made from a steel drum, set up salvaged Army bunk beds made from steel, and located old barrels outside to catch rainwater from the roof.

Rounding out all the essentials of life, finally a rustic outhouse was built quite some distance from the cabin. When nature called at night, it made for a long trek in the eerie, pitch dark! I would hightail it back to the cabin as fast as I could run, fearing wild things that go bump in the night.

There was one very hot and humid summer weekend when Mom and Dad loaded us kids, along with 2,500 tiny tree seedlings, into the station wagon and headed for the country cabin. It was a work weekend that seemed to have no end. Our folks ordered these seedlings through a conservation organization and now they needed to be planted. Whoosh! Down would come the heavy mattock wielded by Dad. The job Al and I had was to take one of the tiny Norway spruce or white pine seedlings and place it in the slit of soil, followed by Mom using her heel to pack the dirt around the seedling roots. It seemed to take a lifetime to plant those trees in the only meadow that covered three acres on our otherwise forested land. The hard labor paid off, with what is a now-towering forest in what was once an open meadow. The quote on the tea bag mentioned earlier comes to mind, "The creation of a thousand forests is in one acorn."

In retrospect, I now know that Dad was creating a haven in case the need arose to survive off the land. Over time, he planted grape vines and fruit trees. Then came the beehives and gleaning the golden honey from them with a homemade extractor. Mom and Dad planted blueberry bushes, chestnut trees, and a vegetable garden. With all the wildlife teaming in the forest and a babbling brook cascading on this land, it is conceivable that we could have survived on what Mother Nature provided.

*   *   *

"The bugles sound retreat, the banners fall,
The host of eager allies melt away.
Many marched bravely with you. Of them all,
Few will stay.
Now fade the cherished hopes that once were bright
Now slowly sinks from sight the dying sun.
Is there an answer in the gathering night?
There is one.
Pick up that broken blade with weary hand.
Shout that this disappearing sun will rise.
Only the lost cause, the last stand,
Wins you the skies!"

--Author Unknown

Chapter 10

The Rest of the Story

*"It is almost impossible for anyone, even the most
ineffective among us, to continue to choose misery after
becoming aware that it is a choice."*
-- William Glasser, 1925

It has been suggested that it takes adversity to shape
your character and you become strengthened through
affliction. I read somewhere that before ore can be refined,
such as with gold, it has to go through a furnace of fire
where the impurities are removed. Dad, sure enough, had
gone through many furnaces of fire and came to that point
of being refined where he chose to be the master of his life
rather than to be mastered by it.

All those years after the war, he was still a prisoner
in his thoughts and it was a prison that could only be
unlocked from the inside. The door to a mental prison will
never open up until a key is tried. One or two keys may not
work, so different keys need to be tried. Perhaps one key
that unlocked Dad's mental prison was plunging himself
into Scouting.

Our entire family became involved in Scouting. I
was in Girl Scouts for ten years, starting out in Brownies at
the age of eight, while Mom was one of our leaders. Dad
started out as a leader for the Cub Scouts and Mom served
as a Den Mother, as well. Al was active in Cub Scouts and
later Boy Scouts, moving all the way up the ranks until he
achieved Eagle Scout. As a Cub Scout leader, and later a
Boy Scout leader for 15 years, Dad found his niche. This
was where he could be a positive influence on young boys,

instilling loyalty and patriotism, while teaching them survival skills.

Top photo: Al, John, and Karen
Bottom photo l to r: Steve Necel, Al, John, Howard Smith, and Craig Brozek

After working all day, Dad would spend his evenings preparing for Scout meetings that would involve hands-on training. He would spend countless hours practicing knot-tying, knife sharpening, compass reading, and just about everything under the sun to make the meetings engaging and educational. He wanted to own the skills before he instructed these youngsters. There was always research to be done, and he would tirelessly glean information from piles of books. He would take out survival filmstrips on loan to be shown with a film projector on a screen, since that is how viewing was done back in those days at Scout meetings. He poured himself into his Scouts, and it became his passion to lead by example.

When it was time for one of the Scouts to interview for advancement in rank, Dad never sugarcoated the experience, as he would grill a nervous boy. One day in particular, a Scout dutifully appeared at our door and was shown to the living room, where he would be questioned in his hope to achieve the rank of First Class. I happened to be hiding around the corner in the kitchen and was eavesdropping. Dad was very formal and asked the candidate to recite the Scout Oath. With a shaking voice the boy replied, "On my honor I will do my best, to do my duty to God and my country and to obey the Scout Law; to help other people at all times; to keep myself physically strong, mentally awake, and morally straight."

When asked if he was reading and studying the Boy Scout Handbook, the Scout said, "Yes, sir." "Hand me your book," Dad instructed. After examining the book, Dad admonished the boy. "How can you tell me you are reading this book? Look, here. The pages are not dog-eared or tattered, the binding isn't broken, and it looks to me like you never even opened the book at all!" That is how Dad would impress upon a boy that this was serious and not to be taken lightly. I swear, that boy probably shook in his pants as he realized he got busted and couldn't pull the wool over his Scoutmaster's eyes! Dad was a force to be reckoned with, and he earnestly lived by the Boy Scout Motto, "Be Prepared."

Reflecting upon his many years in Scouting, Dad said, "I had a good Troop and turned out eight Eagle

Scouts. I trained my kids good and drilled them. They were exposed to camping during all four seasons. At summer camp, I made sure to take the boys to three different churches to worship, whether they were Catholic, Protestant, or Jewish. They were all treated equally and nobody was left out."

Among the many military medals Dad earned, including the Purple Heart, the Combat Infantryman Badge, and the Bronze Star Medal with two Oak Leaf Clusters, he said, "To me, the most important honor above all the others is when I received the Scoutmaster's Key." This key was awarded to those who maintained a quality Scouting program.

Another honor to attest to Dad's commitment to his Scouts was the conferring of the Order of the Arrow title. The Order of the Arrow is Scouting's National Honor Society. It recognizes Scouts who best exemplify the Scout Oath and Law in their daily lives, especially in selfless leadership to help others.

The wallet-sized membership card inscription almost resonates Dad's Army and prisoner of war experiences: *"Because the fellow members of my Scouting unit have selected me as an honor camper and as one who lives according to the Scout Oath or Promise and Law, I will be ever mindful of my obligation always to set a high example for others to follow and to pledge my full service to my unit, doing whatever I can to make it better."*

Troop 192 at Camp Schoellkopf, Cowlesville, NY
Arrow indicates Scoutmaster John Zale

William Shakespeare wrote in Act III of his play Julius Caesar, "The evil that men do lives after them. The good is oft interred with their bones." Not so with Dad. The good that he did for "his Scouts" was still recognized by them many years later after Dad's passing. One powerful testimony came from Paul Sikora, who penned a tribute to his hero when he learned that Dad passed away. The following was read at Dad's funeral:

JOHN ZALE – MY HERO
June 21, 2012

Mr. John Zale was my Head Scoutmaster. Few words can evoke such powerful and positive memories of lessons imparted by this great mentor. The lessons were always positive – "Duty, Honor, Love of Country, and Respect for the Flag" as paramount among many others.

Mr. Zale led by example. You would never have known the ordeals he had been through during the war, by his conduct, and the humble manner in which he carried himself and imparted his lessons to his Scouts. His lessons imparted were best exemplified by the 12 points of the Scout Law:

"TRUSTWORTHY" – I would have trusted the man with my life.

"LOYAL" – No greater example of loyalty to one's country exists.

"HELPFUL" – One of the five most influential persons in my life.

"FRIENDLY" –Despite his experiences, always a friendly disposition to all.

"COURTEOUS" – He was a consummate gentleman to all.

"KIND" – A kinder man could not be found.

"OBEIDIENT" – No greater devotion to duty exists other than his example.

"CHEERFUL" – Always with a smile and good word, despite his ordeals.

"THRIFTY" – Never thrifty with the time he devoted to his Scouts.

"BRAVE" – Bravery beyond words, his actions spoke for themselves.

"CLEAN" – I never remember hearing him swear.

"REVERENT" – His faith in God spoke for itself through his ordeal.

Sleep well, old soldier, may God grant you eternal rest.

For a life filled with good deeds and devotion to flag &
country above all the rest.

You have led by example as few men would have done

And shaped and molded countless young Scouts in so
many ways that were fun.

May God grant you peaceful rest from a lifetime of
good deeds well done.

May good memories remain for all victories won.

May you rest forever – in long eternal, everlasting
peace.

After such a life of service, you deserve this, at the very
least.

With Love and Appreciation,

By Paul Sikora, as "Self-appointed Spokesman for the
Scouts of Troop 192"

Recently, for several hours over coffee, Paul and I had an opportunity to share stories about Dad. As we reminisced, waxing nostalgic, we shared both laughter and tears. The old soldier is gone, but his lessons on life were impactful and still resonated decades later.

One memory I shared was how Dad would discipline the boys when they got out of hand. "Hit the deck and give me 50 pushups," Dad would command. Or, worse yet, the dreaded "dying cockroach!" The misbehaving Scouts would have to lie on their back with legs straight, and raise their feet only four inches off the ground. It wouldn't be long before a stomach ached and weak muscles quivered. The "dying cockroach" lent itself to correcting the miscreants' behavior quickly.

In sharing his thoughts, Paul said, "I remember one time when Troop 192 was 'lining up' at a meeting, and a couple of guys were talking among themselves when the

Pledge of Allegiance was being recited. This was one of the few times I ever saw Mr. Zale 'get angry.' He spoke of the reverence for the flag that he was trying to instill in us all, telling us that 'we should be still, pay attention, and that when we see and think of the flag, the pledge, and National Anthem we should get emotional, get a lump in our throats, and act with reverence.'"

Paul continued, "The one strict rule I remember about meetings was that, under no circumstances, could we break for, or have, water. This was not to punish us, but to teach us discipline, and that sometimes we must 'do without.' In retrospect, he did it to try to 'toughen us up.'

"The only reference he ever made to the war was a very oblique reference, about eating dog meat. I can't remember exactly how it came up, but he said something to the effect that dog meat 'is not that bad,' implying that he had had it at some point during his wartime ordeal. It was not a brag or a boast, but was mentioned very 'matter-of-factly.'

"I never remember Mr. Zale ever swearing. There were only a few times he lost his temper. Mr. Zale was one of the rarest, most gifted leaders, one who lead 'by example' and by his own actions. He 'walked the walk' instead of 'talked the talk.' His examples of patriotism, determination, discipline and love of country have remained with me to this day."

Another Scout, who was influenced by Dad, was Richard Kloch. Richard took his Scouting experience seriously. He, no doubt, honed his leadership skills through Troop 192, where he had the opportunity to serve as the Patrol Leader of the Star Patrol. After hard work and perseverance, Richard achieved the highest honor of Eagle Scout.

When his Scouting years were over, and he pursued a career in law, Richard always stayed in touch with Dad. Dad could not have more proud of "his Scout," who became the North Tonawanda City Judge. Judge Kloch! It didn't stop there, as Richard later became a County Attorney, and, in 2001, became a Court of Claims Judge. Dad would cut out the newspaper clippings of Richard and mail them to me. The icing on the cake was Richard's achieving the esteemed position of New York State Supreme Court Justice. Dad was beaming with pride. Then, much to Dad's surprise and delight, Judge Richard Kloch presided at my marriage to Kerry.

When Dad passed away, Richard came up to me at the funeral. As he paid his respects, he said Dad was a great man. Richard had deep admiration and respect for Dad, as he shared with me, "I am not worthy to even tie his shoe."

There are many more success stories about Dad's Scouts, as he took a keen interest in each and every boy. One Scout, David Wells, became a Major in the Army. Another Scout confided in me after Dad's passing, saying that he lost his father when he was very young. Dad took him under his wing and was like a father to him.

Here we have one man who had such a profound influence on shaping the lives of so many young boys. The Scout Motto, "Be Prepared," was deeply rooted in Dad after all he endured during his youth and wanted that motto to be engrained in each boy. It became part of his legacy. What greater gift can one give, unselfishly of himself, than for the betterment of others. Once again, the Emerson quote on the tea bag tag comes to mind, "The creation of a thousand forests is in one acorn."

Reminiscing about Dad and his love for the outdoors and canoeing, we were young kids when he purchased a 16-

foot-long canvas and wood canoe that he named "The Tamarack." The tamarack was his favorite tree, being the only conifer that loses its needles before winter. The tree first turns a brilliant yellow-gold before shedding its lacey looking needles each autumn.

Dad would slide the sleek canoe into a mirror-still lake, and Al and Dad would then rhythmically paddle us along, as we glided across the glistening water. I would be the lucky passenger, taking in the sights and the occasional sound of the call of a loon. The dragonflies would playfully skim across the top of the water. Those were good times, and Dad was the captain of his soul. Mom would be at the water's edge, watching from the distance, hoping we wouldn't tip over.

Over many decades, time took its toll on the old "Tamarack." When Dad passed away, I transported the canoe to my home in Derby, Vermont. It was in hopeless disrepair (the canoe, not my house), and it took on water when we tried her out in the local lake. She was no longer "sea worthy." Searching through my "catch-all" folder, I located an old ad torn out many years earlier from a magazine. The ad was for a boat builder in New Hampshire, who restores old canvas and wood canoes. Hoping it was still a valid email address, I sent off a message in August of 2013 to see if the canoe could be repaired. I briefly mentioned that my Dad had named this canoe "The Tamarack," and I would like to donate it to the Boy Scouts in his memory.

Not only did I get a response from "Kevin Martin, Boatbuilder," but, much to my shock, he was a tamarack tree enthusiast! Mr. Martin wrote to me:

"I would love to help get the canoe back in good condition, with the name Tamarack on the side, and your

father's story told to all who ask about the canoe. It seems to match me well because I have a strong interest in the tamarack tree as well. I am writing a book about short hikes to the Big Trees of NH and have found several European Larch (tamarack) trees to include. Love the trees though with their golden needles in the fall, and in spring, with new green needles and purple flowers."

I am not a betting woman, but what are the chances of my Dad and Kevin Martin both having their favorite tree be the tamarack! Dad from New York, me living in Vermont, and Mr. Martin building boats in New Hampshire; perhaps God had His hand in this project.

Kevin Martin with the Tamarack before renovation

With a price tag of over $2300 for the renovation, I enlisted the support of former Boy Scouts, family, and friends. They rose to the occasion and generously supported this project with their monetary contributions. Raymond Budnik was the Assistant Patrol Leader of the Rebels Patrol, the same patrol to which Al belonged. In a note Raymond wrote to me, he said:

"Thank you so much for the packet of information on your Dad's life. Your Dad was a great role model for all of us boys in Troop 192. I was especially honored to have known him. He had a great influence on my life. As a parent today, I use many of the ideals he instilled in us as young boys. Please use this small gift to restore his canoe. He would've liked that. The name 'Tamarack' is so fitting. I remembered he loved tamarack trees. (The only pine that drops its needles). Again, Thanks, and God Bless. Sincerely, Raymond Budnik."

Also key to this project was getting the okay from the Boy Scouts of America to accept this canoe as a memorial to Dad. Mr. Russell Etzenhouser, Scout Executive/CEO for the Greater Niagara Frontier Council, graciously offered to permanently house "The Tamarack" at Camp Schoellkopf in Cowlesville, New York. In addition, the donation of the canoe was consented to by the Boy Scouts of America National Foundation located in Irving, Texas. That got the ball rolling!

The time came for "The Tamarack" to make her final "voyage" before being permanently docked. We loaded the canoe on Dad's old 1984 Ford pick-up truck and started the long trek to Epping, New Hampshire. The 29-year old truck had carburetor problems and sputtered over the Green Mountains of Vermont and the White Mountains of New Hampshire. After the renovations were completed six months later, it was time to pick up the canoe. We traveled on a prayer, hoping that the truck would make it to New Hampshire, back again to Vermont, and eventually to Camp Schoellkopf in New York without conking out. Whew! It was a crazy ride, but we made it unscathed.

Karen with The Tamarack preparing for trip to New York
(note "433")

It was quite the undertaking trying to coordinate this project from the hinterland of northern Vermont. Then came a godsend: Ronald Krul. Ron is the Commander of American Legion Post 1451 and Adjutant of the Military Order of the Purple Heart, Chapter 264, in Sanborn, New York. He and Dad were both wounded in action in separate wars and shared that common thread of self-sacrificing service to their fellow man. Ron did not hesitate to offer his time to this project. I must admit, I never could have pulled it off without him.

For starters, who has even heard of an organization called "Bugles Across America?" Ron gave me their website and informed me that they provide a free service for Veterans. Sure enough, I sent out my request and received over a hundred hits for a bugler. One man in particular showed keen interest in playing "Taps" for Dad's dedication ceremony. As it turned out, David Breth was also a Cub Scout Master and asked if he could have the honor of playing the bugle.

After a total of 11 months since this project was started, beginning with the renovation of the canoe, the day came for the ceremony on July 18, 2014. Camp Schoellkopf was holding a closing ceremony that day and over 200 Scouts and parents filled the amphitheater. In addition, there were members from both the Zubrzycki and Antonik sides of the family, friends of the Zales, former Scouts from Dad's troop, Charlie Wells (Dad's Assistant Scoutmaster), Veterans, and an honored guest, Don Griffith, who was a former prisoner of war from WWII.

Ron Krul in front of crowd of Scouts at dedication ceremony

With Ron Krul being the emcee, all the stops were pulled out for this special dedication. After the Boy Scout color guard posted the colors, and the singing of our National Anthem, the camp Chaplain gave the Invocation. Joining me in the staging area were both of Dad's grandchildren, John R. Zale and Katie Zale. After I gave the eulogy, John and Katie presented the canoe to the Executive Director, Mr. Etzenhouser.

The Honorable Richard Kloch was the keynote speaker and was joined center stage by former Scouts from Dad's troop, including John Kloch, Ray Budnik, and Jonathan Kolber. Behind them, two enormous campfires were blazing, crackling, and shooting flames and sparks high into the air. What a fitting setting for these Scouts as they came to honor their Scoutmaster. Judge Kloch delivered a powerful tribute and, in remembering Troop 192, he said in part, "We were strong because we were a unit, we were group. John Zale was on the list of The Greatest Generation and heroes. In their unity they destroyed a monster and won the war over pure evil. He taught us to carry on and do your duty and do it with grace."

There is a special brotherhood that exists among war veterans, and Don Griffith was there to honor his fellow Ex-POW. Mr. Griffith's chapter of the American Ex-POWs, of which Dad was an active member, donated their American parade-flag to the Boy Scouts in the memory of Dad.

Next, Bob Young, the Prisoner of War Group Coordinator from the Veteran's Administration, was able to share a side of Dad that most were not privy to, as he knew about Dad's prison camp history. Bob recounted, "John Zale was very unique and was a survivor. He escaped out of prison camp and then back into the camp to get medical supplies to help his fellow POWs. I know of no other person who has done this. While in China, he was part of Unit 731, where inhumane experiments were done on the men. He did sabotage against the enemy. Later, years after the war, he made a contribution and helped other POWs at the VA Hospital. He took care of the wounded and the sick both during the war and after the war."

To conclude the dedication program, the Scouts conducted a solemn flag-folding ceremony. I donated the flag to the Scouts that was flown over our US Capital in honor of the anniversary date of Dad being wounded in action. Then, slowly, the Scout rifle team raised their guns and delivered a 21-gun salute. As the bugler reverently sounded "Taps," the sun was setting, and there was hardly a dry eye in the crowd.

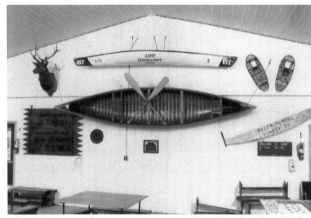

The Tamarack on permanent display in the dining hall at Camp Schoellkopf

Looking back a couple of decades, the time finally came when Dad handed over the torch of Troop 192 and was no longer immersed in Scouting. Both Al and I were adults and on our own paths, leaving Mom and Dad as "empty-nesters." At one point, when questioned about how he dealt with the painful past he said, "The secret to the whole thing is work. You can't be idle. After the war I had to work to keep my sanity. I poured myself into hard, physical work. I never talked about my story." That escape through hard work was soon to change.

When Dad turned 60 in 1982, he retired after 31 years working as a civil servant for the federal government. With no work, Scouting, or raising kids to occupy his mind, the memories of combat and imprisonment reared their ugly heads. These soldiers returned home traumatized and the horrors stayed with them forever. The damage is permanent. It could be likened to when you experience a severe, deep cut. The bleeding stops and the wound heals over superficially, but the ugly scar remains forever. Without the distraction of keeping himself constantly occupied, his mind was now insidiously focusing on the scars.

Over the next two years, Mom became deeply concerned about the changes she saw in his behavior as he became withdrawn. She knew her husband needed help and insisted he go to the VA. When interviewed at the VA, he said that Stella was his best friend and that, no doubt, was the impetus for him to follow her urging.

Again, that was monumental to saving his sanity from the tormenting demons. In 1984, he became a founding member of the Western New York Chapter of the American Ex-Prisoners of War, at the age of 62. It wasn't until all these years later that Mom finally learned what Dad had gone through during the war and what he had been inwardly battling for 39 years. The time came when he shared his dark past with her, much to her shock. She often wondered what it was that she did (or didn't do), that was causing his behavior, and now she understood. A heavy weight was lifted off her shoulders as she got a glimpse into a side of her husband that she never knew existed. Her tears flowed.

Over the years, the swirling, bitter concoction of continual hunger, malnutrition, disease, slave labor, mental and physical abuse was served up to Dad and manifested itself as severe anxiety disorder. Very often, combat veterans find it difficult to talk about what they saw during the war or how they feel about it. It gets locked up inside and these feelings keep getting bottled up. The impact of going to the VA support group was like medicine for Dad. It became a weekly dose of wellness for him as he gathered with other former prisoners of war. It was here where they could share their stories that no one else could possibly understand.

Recently, I spoke with Bob Young, the VA POW Group Coordinator in Buffalo, New York. Speaking about the men in this group he said, "They felt they had an obligation to do something good to exemplify the virtue of 'giving back.' They knew that freedom also means 'Americanism' and being responsible to other people. Your dad participated in the Speakers Bureau, going to local schools as an inspiration to the students. He also volunteered every week at the VA Medical Center, at the corner of Main Street and Hertel Avenue, making and distributing coffee to veterans." It was this inherent need to keep helping others and not dwelling on himself that was the saving grace to Dad's mental well-being.

Left to right: Paul Feigenbaum, John Zale, Bob MacPherson, Stan Blake, serving coffee

Two more "saints" were sent to Dad's rescue: Eli Pollinger and Barbara Wolfrum, both who worked for the Veterans Administration. The crossing of their paths was deeply impactful on all three. Dad had the utmost respect and highest regard for Eli and Barbara, as these two individuals were devoted to serving the POWs.

Eli Pollinger was the Ex-POW Coordinator at the Buffalo VA Medical Center. In 1992, he conducted a POW Social Survey when Dad was 70 years old. Eli readily determined that Dad had Post-Traumatic Stress Disorder (PTSD). This was manifested with anxiety, horrible nightmares, flashbacks, and reclusive behavior. There were memory lapses and episodes of profuse perspiration. Dad felt his experience of three and one-half years of Japanese imprisonment didn't really happen to him, as if it were all a bad dream.

Mom was also at the interview, and she shared with Eli that her husband avoided people, was totally suspicious, and paranoid. He didn't let anyone come into the house and would not socialize. He spent unusual amounts of time by himself in the woods, avoided crowds, and was hyper-vigilant.

Eli was a tireless champion for the rights of the POWs. He worked diligently to get these patriots 100% service-connected disability. In a nutshell, in 1957, Dad received a letter from the VA that his condition had "improved," and they were reducing his service-connected disability from 30% to 10%. Try to comprehend all of this as a former POW, who was put through the crucible in incomprehensible ways as he served his country, being told that his condition improved. Eventually, over 30 years later, he received a letter in 1989 that his disability compensation was increased to 60%. Ultimately, through great effort and energy on the part of Eli, it was finally acknowledged that these men deserved nothing less than 100% disability compensation.

The Ex-POW group at the Buffalo VA Medical Center. Arrows indicate Eli Pollinger (l) and John Zale (r)

Barbara Wolfrum, a Clinical Social Worker at the VA, was Dad's therapist and treated him for PTSD. She had the remarkable gift that allowed her to penetrate the shroud that concealed Dad's past. He was able to open up and tell her what had been hidden deep within him for so many painful years. It was at Barbara's urging and her counseling that she convinced Dad to tell me the stories, as well.

Just recently, I spoke with Barbara, as we shared stories about Dad. She said, "John would regularly volunteer at the VA and obtain a list of veterans who were hospitalized. He would then go visit with each and every one of them. That is what your dad did, he was always helping people." My response was, "It was Dad's way of dealing with his PTSD and getting out of his own head, by immersing himself in others." Barbara concurred. Dad told me that there were only two people besides family that he sent cards to and they were Barbara and Eli. He considered them to be his loyal and dearest friends.

To fast-forward momentarily, Dad was still volunteering at the VA every week at the age of 90. He even visited with the veterans at the VA just two days before his passing. I found a certificate that Dad had received two months before he passed, dated April 18, 2012. It was a "VA Health Care Certificate of Achievement" for 15 Years and 4,253 Hours of Voluntary Service."

On another note, the VA "day center" offered different classes. You could call it therapy, or perhaps it was meant as an opportunity to enjoy a hobby. Besides woodworking, Dad engrossed himself in the attention-challenging art of stained glass. As he concentrated on the details of cutting glass, adding foil, and welding, he created lampshades, wall clocks and hundreds of sun-catchers. The single-most thought provoking sun-catcher that reflected his past was that of a "red sail in the sunset." The song that he heard as he was shipping out from the United States to go to the Philippine Islands in April of 1940 was "Red Sails in the Sunset." This was an attestation of a pleasant memory he was able to conjure up.

During one interview, Eli asked, "What would you tell our servicemen and women today?" Dad thoughtfully replied, "Be glad you can serve your country. It gives you a different outlook on life. The guys coming home are going to need help. The most important thing is that they need a job and need to work. Keep yourself worn out in order not to think about the war years."

Over the years, Dad became increasingly involved with other veterans. Besides the American Ex-POW group, he became active with the Military Order of the Purple Heart local chapter. When it was time to gather for the annual summer picnic, Dad would don a chef's hat and apron and cook sizzling hotdogs for his fellow patriots. He always brought a big, juicy watermelon that he would take a machete to, for a refreshing treat.

Top: Cooks John Zale and Henry Pacer; Bottom: Ex-POW 433
license plate

Don Meckle and John Zale manning an Ex-POW booth

What follows is a brief summation of what, in and of itself, could fill the pages of a book. If there is one word that would describe Dad, it would be loyalty. He was bound by duty to his fellow patriots and was completely devoted to his family and his Scouts. So, it shouldn't come as a surprise that a very unique and enduring pact was formed that underscored his loyalty. The sworn members of this pact were John and Stella Zale and Joe and Risa Fragale. Both men survived the Bataan Death March.

There is a rich history behind the story of Risa (Rechter) Fragale. She was a Jewish woman born in Vienna, Austria. The dark cloud of evil was forming on the horizon with the ineluctable approach of Hitler's Nazis. The year was 1936. Risa was 14 years old when the Rechter family left Austria. Due to the Nazi persecution of the Jews, the Rechters became a family without a country. Over the next three years, their journey to seek refuge took them from Italy, to Japan, then to Shanghai, and lastly to Manila in the Philippine Islands.

It was while Risa was in the Philippines that she met Joseph Fragale. It was somewhat of a Hollywood story: Here in the tropical islands, Risa, a beautiful 17-year-old Jewish woman from Austria, met the debonair Joe. Joe was a Catholic from Buffalo, New York, who was stationed at Nichols Field, near Manila, in the 5th United States Air Force. The handsome couple fell in love and married in August 1941. Life was happy for these newlyweds, until four months later with the bombings by the Japanese on Pearl Harbor and Nichols Field, where Joe was posted.

Alas, an ominous ill wind was sweeping over the Pearl of the Orient. With tension in the air, Joe took Risa to her parent's home in Manila. Soon thereafter, there was an air raid on Nichols Field and the Japanese destroyed the house in which Joe and Risa had been living. On Christmas Day, Joe, Risa, and her parents had dinner together. Joe got the call to immediately report to duty and, at that same moment, Risa informed her husband that she was pregnant.

When the American and Filipino forces were surrendered to the Japanese in April of 1942, both my Dad and Joe Fragale started their hellish ordeal on the Bataan Death March. Both were to become prisoners of war for three and one-half years. Meanwhile, in Manila, Risa gave birth to Joseph Fragale, Jr. in July of 1942, and father and son would not see each other until after the war ended.

In 1945, Risa and her young child departed by ship to the United States, with a final destination of Buffalo, New York. With the war ending, Joe Fragale, Sr. finally returned home to Buffalo in October of 1945 and saw his son for the first time. Just a few miles south of Buffalo, fellow survivor, John Zubrzycki, returned home in December of that same year.

It wasn't until the late 1980s that the Zales and the Fragales became close friends through the American Ex-POW group. That is when the pact was formed. Each individual's personal experiences were worlds apart, yet the lives of these four people were inextricably intertwined. As their life's journey continued, it was agreed that if one member passed on, the others would look after each other.

In 1995, Mom was losing her battle to breast cancer. She asked Joe and Risa, "Will you be sure to watch over John? I'm concerned for his well-being after I'm gone." When she passed, Eli Pollinger gave her eulogy. Dad lost his best friend. The pact now had three loyal members. The three remained true to their friendship and looked out after one another. However, just one year later, in 1996, Joe had to face reality before his passing and asked Dad, "John, please take care of my Risa. I don't want her to be alone."

The vow had been made years ago, and the pact was still honored. Dad told me that he promised Joe that he would watch over Risa, and he kept that promise of loyalty. At this point, both Dad and Risa were 74 years old and, dealing with life in their advanced years, offered each other support. For the next 15 years, Dad checked in on Risa, took her grocery shopping, and they still had conversations about the Philippine Islands of yore. The time came when Risa needed advanced medical care. Her son arranged for his mother to be moved to South Carolina. Later that same year, Dad passed on. Once again, dear family friend, Eli Pollinger, gave the eulogy. All four of these loyal friends lived up to their pact right until the end.

While engaged in writing this book, it was with a heavy heart that I received word that Risa had passed at age 95. On February 27, 2018, family and friends gathered at her graveside. Having never been to a Jewish ceremony such as this, I was unaware of the customs. After Risa's coffin was lowered into the ground, each of us who were in attendance was asked to come forward to participate in her interment. Hesitantly, I slowly approached a mound of dirt, in which several shovels were imbedded. Taking hold of one of the long wooden handles, I scooped up some of the earth. Then, ever so gently, I turned the shovel sideways and the earth slipped off the shovel's end, onto the coffin. It was so poignant and so final. Now, all four of the members of the pact are resting within yards of each other at the same cemetery.

Back in the early days, while we were still together as a family, Mom was the stalwart with boundless energy. Her heart overflowed with love and she was a delight to be around. She would light up a room with her vivacious personality and, honestly, everybody loved her. She was Dad's anchor in his sea of tumultuous emotions. He would say that she was one in a million. That she was.

After her passing, I would make the drive from my home in Vermont to spend time with Dad. There was a noticeable emptiness in the house, a gaping hole that existed, after all those years that was once filled by Mom. Dad was in his mid-70s and I was already 45 years old when he finally told me the stories of his war- time experience. This was 50 years after the war. As a result of years of counseling with his confidant, Barbara Wolfrum, and her exhortation to share his stories with his family, he came to grips with the need to share his dark past with me.

It would be in the late evening, Dad sitting in his worn, dark brown recliner. An end table and lamp separated us, as I sat in the empty chair. The soft light from the lamp emphasized the deep lines on his face, carved by time. The effects of the war went far deeper than the skin. It seeped into every fiber of his being. When he would begin to open up and talk about being a POW, his face would transform and there was a distinct distance in his eyes. The eyes are the doorway to the soul. The tone of his voice became very quiet and subdued, yet steady. His speech was slow and deliberate. As his mind was transported back to another world, the mist of time enveloped him as he relived those moments. At times, while talking, he would wince and have a pained expression that came over his face, yet he never shed a tear.

"Oh, mój Kashu," he would say affectionately in Polish for "my Karen." "I can't put this all together in any kind of sequence. I can't put it in story form," he would explain. "How can anybody believe what happened when I can't believe I went through this myself. It was like a bad nightmare. You don't really know what freedom is until you lose it."

Quietly, I would sit there, trying to absorb all that he was sharing. It was numbing to hear it. There were two stories that must have been profoundly impactful on him, as he told them repeatedly. First was the story of his POW buddy who asked Dad to trade his smaller bag for the musette bag. This was the man who attempted to escape, was caught, and murdered in front of the POWs. The second story was that of being in solitary confinement for two weeks in a small box, watching a spider weave a web in order to keep his sanity.

He also shared, "I had 'survivor's guilt.' Why did I get to survive and return home while so many others didn't? Mothers never got to see their sons again. Why me? But I loved my country so much I would do it all over again if I had to fight once more for my country. We came back home from the war feeling like our country didn't owe us anything. We just did our patriotic duty."

As the hands of time whirled ever so quickly and the years ticked by, Dad continued to share his war stories during these special moments. One evening in particular as he spoke, we were both cracking open a bucketful of acorns that I had picked in Vermont. Acorns are a wonderful survival food, packed with tons of nourishing fat. After we cracked acorns all evening, I leached out the tannins, and dried the nutmeat overnight. The next day, it was time to pulverize the dried acorns in a coffee bean grinder, yielding flour to bake a "survival" coffee cake for Dad. In addition, I brewed some tea from white pine tree needles, which is very high in vitamin C. He knew he taught his daughter well. The old soldier needn't worry if his little girl could take care of herself.

On a lighter note, we laughed over how he had another nickname for me besides Kashu or Kashka. When I would get under his skin as a young girl, he would call me "gnida," in Polish, which loosely translates to "flea egg." Hopefully, the real meaning got lost in the translation! Then, referring to our relationship, Dad said, "The nut doesn't fall too far from the tree."

As a little girl, Dad would take Al and me camping. He was always teaching us skills to be independent. The long walks through the woods to learn what plants were edible and those that could heal all had a purpose. It wasn't just "entertainment" for his two children. These were lessons to be imbedded in us if the time ever came to put them to use. Now, I am able to understand how he was shaping us to "Be Prepared." Having him as a role model all my life, I became fiercely independent. As a single adult, I took trips by myself and I thought it odd when people asked me, "Who did you go with on the trip?" Who? It never occurred to me to ask anyone to go with me!

These included a trip to Hawaii, where I hiked a remote rain forest on the island of Kaua'i and took in the magnificent grandeur of the Na Pali Coast. There was a brief moment of panic when I got lost in this very remote area, losing the almost indiscernible footpath for a short distance. No wonder the books I read in preparation of this hike said to never hike alone. Luckily, there were no encounters with any of the large-tusked wild boar about which they warned. Heck! Nobody back in Buffalo, New York, even knew I was gone.

Equally as magical was a solo trip to hike in Alaska. The state's wilderness is so spectacular that it puts one on sensory overload, but one must use common sense when hiking alone. A tip-off was a sign at the entrance of a hiking trail at Chugach State Park/Potter Creek. It somberly stated, "Alaska's vast wilderness is big enough to shelter more than 98 percent of the US population of brown bears, also called grizzlies." Oh, sure, grizz. That was the fastest day hike I ever took in my life!

Flexing my independence muscles was cut short while I was at the airport ready to fly to France. I made all the reservations to see Paris on my own and then hike in the Pyrenees Mountains in the south of France. The world came to a screeching halt that day, September 11, 2001. Sitting in the airport in Montreal, Quebec, with all flights cancelled, the trip was abruptly terminated. Being a Federal Law Enforcement Officer for Homeland Security, I was ordered back to the northern border in Vermont.

The point of the above-mentioned details of traveling solo, is that it was the influence of my father that I found a passion in learning survival skills. It is no surprise, as the daughter of a former prisoner of war, that I walked in his shadow. Dad did cast a large shadow. I describe both myself and Al as "reclusive." We shun parties and crowds.

Both of us have zero interest in social media. Spending time walking in peacefulness of the forest Dad left me sure beats following the crowd. Poet Robert Frost said in "The Road Not Taken," "Two roads diverged in a wood, and I—I took the one less traveled by, and that has made all the difference." Be assured, if the crowd is going to the left, you will find me going to the right.

I have a core of very close friends, yet my comfort zone is spending quality time with only one person at a time. Apparently, the saying, "Two is company and three is a crowd," suits me to a tee. Despite our self-acknowledged contentment with being reclusive, both Al and I follow Dad's example by volunteering to help others. Isn't that why we have been put on this planet, simply to offer a helping hand?

To those of us who have lived with a war veteran, or those who feel the effects of having seen others who suffered trauma (such as first-responders), it was explained to me that certain attitudes and actions are made manifest due to "vicarious PTSD." It is also referred to as "secondary PTSD."

It was just by chance that I had an epiphany and was made aware of actions of the subconscious. It was in July of 2014, during a trip to Buffalo from my home in Vermont, that Eli and Cathy Pollinger invited me for a visit to their home. The conversation naturally was spent mostly talking about Dad. Their daughter, Sarah, shared her feelings about "Mr. John." She said, "When we received word that Mr. John died, we were all devastated. He was like family to us, and he was like a grandfather to me. Mr. John never missed a family function, even attending our graduations."

At some point, Eli inquired about survival skills that Dad had instilled in me. The response I gave made reference to the popular credit card slogan, "Never Leave

Home Without It,"-- I never, ever am without a magnesium striker. Huh? What? Eli pressed for more details. To explain, I went into my purse and pulled out the fire-making tool, an old "film canister," and a folding knife. They are my constant companions. He asked for a demonstration. Taking out a cotton ball that had been saturated in petroleum jelly from the film canister, I placed it on a flat surface. Next, with the knife, I made shavings of magnesium from the tool, and piled it on the cotton ball. At this point, without actually starting a fire in the middle of their living room, I explained the next step. Striking the knife on the metal rod attached to the tool, a spark readily ignites the magnesium-covered cotton ball and gives you a few minutes of a ball of fire on which to pile tinder.

The conversation continued with a story about a wilderness survival course I attended in New Hampshire with nine men from various parts of the United States. I was the only female. It rained the entire weekend. Our instructor gave each of us only one match, and we were to individually build a fire. The forest was soaking wet. Lessons learned from Dad during my youth led me to gather tinder that was dry underneath tree branches, and there was a mother lode of pinesap that was the saving grace. Slathering the pinesap on the pile of tinder was all it took to ignite a huge ball of flames with only one match! Not one of the men was able to pull it off. The more survival knowledge you carry in your head, the less you have to carry on your back. Dad was the ideal teacher. He knew about survival.

After discussing the survival "bug-out" bag I travel with, Eli exclaimed, "These are all indicators that you are displaying 'vicarious PTSD' resulting from living with a former ex-prisoner of war." Eli was perspicacious due to his training and experience, and he readily honed in on the apparent result of Dad's influence in my life. For those who are in this same situation, who have either been traumatized or have seen horrible things, the people who live with these survivors are directly influenced by their behavior. Post-traumatic stress syndrome needs to be communicated to help both the person directly affected and those around him or her. Knowledge is power. Talking about the past painful events and concomitant feelings are a conduit to understanding.

In November of 1942, the survivor of the Bataan Death March and the Hell Ship was given his prisoner of war number. As John stood shivering in the no-man's land of Mukden, Manchuria, his identity became a number. Number **433**. Dad identified with that number until he breathed his last breath on earth. The faces of his Japanese tormentors never left him. In the Japanese language, "papa san" means "father." During all those years of growing up as the daughter of a prisoner of war, I never grasped the reason why he would always sign birthday or Christmas cards to me with, "Your papa san—**433**." He didn't sign the cards with "Dad." The number **433** was his indelible identity. Now it became apparent, after all these decades later, that this was an attestation to the permanent scars tattooed to his memory.

DEAR KASHU! —
   A EARLY BIRTHDAY TO
YOU. A HAPPY "51" AND YOU
THINK THAT'S OLD. WAIT
TILL YOU GET TO "81" LIKE
PAPASAN: — ENJOY YOUR
BIRTHDAY IT COMES BUT
ONCE A YEAR. YOU ARE A
GREAT DAUGHTER, I'M GLAD
THAT YOUR MINE.
                I REMAIN YOUR
                PAPA SAN
P.S.   "433"
ENJOY THIS
SMALL GIFT.

There's no greater joy than a daughter —
She brings such delight when she's small,
And, when she grows up, she's so special —
She's one of your best friends of all.
She's someone to be very proud of,
She's someone to love a lot, too,
There's no greater joy than a daughter —
Especially a daughter like you!

Happy Birthday

A daughter's a treasure
who, right from the start,
Takes over your home,
your life and your heart...

A daughter's a wonder—
a sweet mixture of
Pleasure and problems,
laughter and love...

A daughter's a gift
and a dream that's come true—
She's someone to cherish
your whole lifetime through.

You're a wonderful
daughter —
and that's always
meant so much.

Merry Christmas
MY DEAR DAUGHTER! —
   I'M GLAD YOU ARE YOURSELF.
I'M GLAD THAT YOU CAN TAKE CARE
OF YOURSELF. YOU NEVER
GAME ME ANY TROUBLE. YOU
ARE A GOOD DAUGHTER AND
I'M HAPPY THAT YOU ARE MINE.
            THANK YOU
            MERRY CHRISTMAS
            PA PA SAN
            "433"

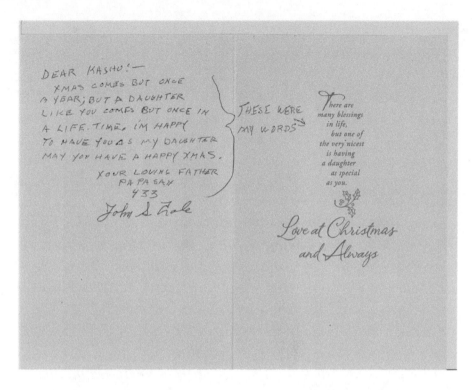

DEAR KASHU! —
XMAS COMES BUT ONCE A YEAR; BUT A DAUGHTER LIKE YOU COMES BUT ONCE IN A LIFE. TIME. I'M HAPPY TO HAVE YOU AS MY DAUGHTER MAY YOU HAVE A HAPPY XMAS.
YOUR LOVING FATHER
PAPA SAN
433

John S. Cole

THESE WERE MY WORDS

There are many blessings in life, but one of the very nicest is having a daughter as special as you.

Love at Christmas and Always

Some of the survivors of the Death March managed to stay in contact to a certain extent upon their return home after the war. Among Dad's papers that I found after he passed was a letter from Abie Abraham, who rescued Dad while he lay wounded on the battlefield. The letter in part reads:

"Dear John. Good hearing from you. I have been intending to write you. My wife died about five years ago. She was an internee in the Philippines, probably you have seen her. Not much left of the old 31st or C Company. It was a good outfit. John, if I'm not mistaken, I believe I helped carry you off the Abucay line when you were wounded in the stomach. Abie."

Abie Abraham went on to write a book entitled, "Ghost of Bataan Speaks." Now in my mid-sixties, I just read this book. It is very gut-wrenching, but it gives great insight into what Dad and his fellow prisoners of war endured.

Another letter I came upon was written one year before the passing of my mother. It was from a former POW, Jack Williams, from New Jersey. He wrote in part:

"Stella, your John was a rock in some very bleak days as a P.O.W. We were taken prisoner against our will. We did not quit – rather our officer corp (the ones on top) quit. They were so busy having a good time in Manila before the war that they forgot to become good officers. It was Sgts. like Zubrzycki who kept the troops alive. By the way, I never got as cold in Korea as I did in Manchuria. Can you imagine trying to make burnable bricks out of coal dust and clay – pretty dumb! As to apologizing to the Japs, I apologize to my dog for the way I treated the Manchurian dogs. Respectfully yours, Jack. John used to say to me 'dubra notes' excuse spelling." ("Dobranoc" is Polish for "good night.")

Stories have been told of some former POWs who received emotional relief after forgiving their former captors. Dad was not so forgiving. When asked if he could forgive the Japanese, his bitter reply was, "Gimme a Jap to keep down in my basement for three and one-half years and I'll think about it."

The stories Dad shared with both Al and me over the years, along with the piles of documents and letters found in Dad's room after he passed, led to the pages contained in this book. One more item that was found was an article dated July 2011. It was about an annual event held every March. I had no knowledge of this, but now it became of extreme interest to me. Why didn't Dad ever tell us about this gathering?

In the dry, hot desert northeast of Las Cruces, New Mexico, over 6,000 people participate in the Bataan Memorial Death March every year. Having participated in over 150 road races myself, this was worth looking into. The website described this as a commemoration to those men who were forced on the Bataan Death March in 1942, which is held on the White Sands Missile Range. The warnings are stern to those who wish to be challenged by either the 14.2-mile or 26.2-mile course on this Army base. The majority of those who take on this challenge are current or former members of the military.

The weather is a factor, with chilly temperatures at the pre-dawn start, which quickly go up to over 100 degrees in the dry desert heat. It is advised to bring a bandana or scarf as a face-cover due to the strong wind blowing sand in your eyes, mouth, and face. It is advised to wear supportive boots or shoes due to the areas of the course that meander through ankle-deep sand, lending to ankle twisting, falls, and blisters.

Add to that, warnings of poisonous snakes, scorpions, and other creepy-crawlies should be noted. Protect your skin from the scorching sun. Have a plan in case you need to be medically evacuated. Stick to the designated path due to areas that are potentially contaminated with explosive devices. With all these warnings, it became apparent why Dad didn't inform me about this memorial march.

Sign for Bataan Memorial Death March at White Sands
Missile Range, New Mexico

Any normal-thinking person would shun the thought of participating in such an event. Nonetheless, after applying online, it occurred to me that, in the dead of winter, the frozen tundra of northern Vermont doesn't lend itself to training properly. January and February found me covered in multi-layers of thermal underwear worn under a snorkel parka, as I ventured out to train in below-zero wind-chill temperatures. The casual observer would think I was preparing to summit Mount Everest.

It isn't exactly desert sand, but the deeply rutted snow and frozen furrows somewhat simulated the uneven surfaces to be confronted in New Mexico. As I slugged through the snow, the water bottle would freeze, and the ice-cold M&M's were similar to biting down on rocks on these training hikes. As children, Dad would impress upon us to never say, "I can't." I tried not to say, "I can't do this," while making two continuous five-mile laps around Echo Lake in East Charleston, Vermont, for a total of 10 miles. Ten miles should be close enough to the 14.2 miles to be hiked in New Mexico. This went on for two months. My head was wrapped in a woolen scarf, not to keep blowing sand out of my face, but to keep my face from turning blue and relatively thawed, despite the frigid winds.

How ludicrous is it to think that training in deep snow and below-freezing temperatures, could prepare one for the challenge of the Bataan Memorial Death March in desert sand and searing heat. Dad's mantra, "Never say, 'I can't'," resonated in my head, however. Thankfully, the march was successful. Now, I continue to train in the dead of winter in Franklinville, New York, on snow-covered country roads, all bundled up against the elements.

It is a moving experience to be marching with over 6,000 participants, mostly young military men and women. Very few of us are descendants of those dauntless men who straggled along the road in the Philippine Islands with the specter of death gripping at every step. The degree of difficulty of marching along the dusty path on the White Sands Missile Range pales in comparison to what those Death Marchers endured. There is no comparison whatsoever.

Marchers supporting the Wounded Warriors

Bataan Memorial Death March (Bottom photo: Author Karen Zale in foreground)

Over 6,000 marchers stretching for miles through the White Sands Missile Range, New Mexico

We gather once each year to come and honor those men, and to remember their sacrifice of fighting for our many freedoms. As I cross the finish line, the tears start to flow down a dust-covered face and chills come over my body. Thoughts of Dad overwhelm me. Had he not crossed the proverbial "finish line," I would not have been born to share in his legacy. He had the *will to survive* the unknown fate that lay before him.

There were also men and women crossing the finish line of this memorial march who were wounded warriors, with prosthetic legs and arms. Lives and limbs have not been spared in the fight for liberty. All 6,000 of us unified marchers were a moving testament to what freedom means, as we paid homage to the sacrifice so many have made to secure our precious freedom.

Over several years, there was the weekly habit of calling Dad from Vermont every Wednesday and every weekend. We had the usual chit-chat about how the garden was growing or about the weather. It was a hot, sunny Sunday in June of 2012 and time for the usual phone call. This was Father's Day and I dialed the number for my "papa san." After several phone calls with no answer, my concern was shared with Al. "Al, could you just take a spin over to Dad's house? He hasn't been answering his phone all day." Living almost 500 miles away caused me to worry a bit if Dad was okay.

Al drove to Dad's house. The back door was open. When Dad stepped outside earlier on that Father's Day morning, he didn't walk back inside. He was in his backyard, under a tree, where his heart had beat for the last time. The faithful servant had been called to rest.

After making the dreaded phone call to 9-1-1, Al went into the house to get a blanket that Dad kept draped over the back of the couch. It had a design of an American flag with an eagle and the words, "Freedom is Not Free." Solemnly, Al covered the old soldier with this patriotic blanket, reflecting that Dad paid the price for our freedom and it is not free. Respectfully, Al walked over to the flag pole, as he slowly lowered the beautiful American flag to half-staff. For "**433**" the battle is finally over.

*   *   *

FREEDOM IS NOT FREE

I watched the Flag pass by one day,
It fluttered in the breeze,
A young cadet saluted it,
And then he stood at ease,
I looked at him in uniform
So young, so tall and proud.
With hair cut square and eyes alert,
He'd stand out in any crowd.
I thought how many men like him
Had fallen through the years,
How many had died on foreign soil?
How many mothers tears?
How many zoomies planes shot down?
How many squids died at sea?
How many foxholes were soldiers graves?
No, freedom is not free.
I wonder just how many times
That Taps had meant "Amen"
When a flag had covered a coffin,
Of a soldier and a friend.
I thought about a graveyard,
At the bottom of the sea,
Of unmarked graves at Arlington,
No, freedom is not free.

Epilogue

Isaiah 55:11 "So shall my word be that goeth forth out of my mouth: it shall not return unto me void, but it shall accomplish that which I please, and it shall prosper in the thing whereto I sent it."

It has been a seemingly impossible task to tell my Dad's story, and it was quite overwhelming to write. A seed was planted, and the gestation stage was long and uncomfortable, followed by birth pangs, ad nauseum.

Dad was larger than life, and he comes alive once again through this book that tells his story. *The Will to Survive* is part of his continuing legacy, which is one of deep loyalty to serving his fellow patriots, his family, and the community.

The purpose of this book is for you, the reader, to grasp the enormity of the trials and struggles the prisoners of war endured to just survive at the most basic level. Moreover, the story tells of how one man was able to deal with his post-war life and Post-Traumatic Stress Disorder (PTSD).

Americans tend to take their freedoms for granted. The men and women of our armed forces paid the price to secure our freedom from tyrannical forces. There is so much that has never been told. Only those who went through this experience can tell it--in order for us to better understand the trauma they endured both during and after the war. Those of us who are descendants need to tell of the experiences of our fathers to prevent their untold stories from being interred with their bodies.

A caveat is essential at this point. I am not a psychologist or a counselor. I am just a daughter of a soldier who lived with PTSD. This is his story and perhaps the reader may find inspiration. Being the daughter of a former POW, I emphatically implore anyone who has seen combat, is conflicted, or otherwise experienced trauma to tell their family about it. Talk about it. If for no other reason, the family needs to understand their loved one's actions, and not to blame themselves for believing they are doing something wrong.

The POWs lost control of their lives during captivity and were stripped of all freedom, but the Japanese could never take control of the prisoners' souls and their *will to survive*. These men wanted to live. My Dad could have given in to the hopelessness, stopped trying, and quit. In the aftermath, it is easier to give in to depression and anxiety than to stand up to it. If you lose hope, you stop caring.

Perhaps you are on this planet to lessen the misery in this world because of what you endured. Making small decisions can influence the larger problems in life. Earth-shattering contributions don't have to be made, but absolutely any small contribution can be meaningful to both the giver and the recipient.

My Dad's advice to those dealing with the deeply rooted injury of PTSD would be to stay active and work hard. It could be to volunteer. Call a buddy. Find a purpose in life in which you can immerse yourself. These are choices my Dad made that saved his sanity. Then, in turn, he was a positive influence on so many others. He did it humbly and took no credit for it.

Nobody has had the exact life experience and don't expect people to understand what you went through. No one has walked in your shoes. Talk it out with others who went through a similar experience. Share your journey. Make an effort to replace despair with hope and replace defeat with faith. Don't go it alone. We have been designed by our Creator to be happy and not hopeless.

The lines on these pages are a reflection of the furrowed lines engraved on Dad's face caused by trial and tribulation. He continued to fight an internal war buried deep within the recesses of his mind. It was through disassociation from the trauma that he was able to call it "a bad dream."

In Chapter 9, it was mentioned how Dad was like the Energizer Bunny personified, and he just kept going and going. No doubt, he still has not stopped in an effort to reach out and help others. His life's story is a testament to that. It is Staff Sergeant Zubrzycki's modus operandi. To you, the reader, he is still reaching out. In conclusion, the message of his story is about hope, about a brighter future, and about choices. Perhaps his will to survive morphed into the will to continue.

If you would like to share your thoughts with me, you are welcomed to do so. I can be reached by email at willtosurvive433@yahoo.com.

*   *   *

No mama, no papa, and **still** no Uncle Sam

Acknowledgments

Three unexpected events led to the writing of this biography. As a descendent of a survivor of the Bataan Death March, I joined The American Defenders of Bataan and Corregidor Memorial Society. In May of 2016, I attended their annual convention, which was held in San Antonio, Texas. My path crossed that of Margaret Garcia, a daughter of another survivor.

Margaret Garcia had written a book about her father, Evans Garcia, entitled "Tell Me Another War Story." She was at a location designated as the "Book Store/Gift Area," selling her book. After having purchased her book, she mentioned that she noticed I was wearing a necklace with a cross. Inquiring if I was a Christian, I replied in the affirmative. Margaret then impressed upon me the importance of our telling the stories of our fathers, who were survivors of the Death March and prison camp. I filed that proposed undertaking in the back of my grey matter upon returning home from the convention.

A week later, out of the clear blue, I received a phone call from Eli Pollinger, who delivered the eulogy for both of my parents. It was nearly four years ago, in 2014, that we had a conversation at his home regarding the "vicarious PTSD" I displayed with my obsession of survival skills. I was taken aback by Eli's purpose of this phone call. He strongly suggested I write a book about my father teaching me survival skills. "Certainly, you jest," is the thought that went through my mind at such an implausible suggestion. Heck, working for the Department of Justice, and, later for the Department of Homeland Security, the only ability I had for writing was quoting sections of law that pertained to brief descriptions of violations of Federal law for the offenders I encountered. The KISS principle applied--"Keep It Simple, Stupid," while penning reports. Verbose prose was not encouraged.

As I pooh-poohed the absurd idea of writing a book and the improbability of even the remote possibility of such a pursuit, a few days later the phone rang. It was my neighbors, and dear friends, Cathy and Dick Haberer. Lo and behold, they informed me of an opportunity being offered by our local library in Franklinville, New York. The Blount Library was offering assistance for first-time authors to publish their book. Lastly, the icing on the cake was a prayer at church that Sunday when Pastor Dan prayed, "Inspire the work and words of authors.....and for advocates who speak for the voiceless." There was no backing out now. The marching orders came through loudly and clearly to be a voice for the voiceless.

A sincere thank you to the wonderful folks at the Blount Library who made this undertaking become a reality. Specifically, Don Watkins, Jessie Frank, and Kim Whitling, who offered countless hours of support.

A debt of gratitude is owed to Al Zale for his input, insight, and co-editing. Dad shared his stories with both of us at different times. We corroborated these stories, thus confirming their veracity. "Thank you" to co-editor Michael Spitz for his expertise and volunteering his time to this project. It was paramount to have a second set of eyes to see this story from the standpoint of someone who did not know Dad. His suggestions were invaluable.

Another blessing sent to assist with this project was Tiffany Smith. Tiffany created the book cover and illustrated the maps. She listened intently to what was needed, did extra research on her own, and her creativity was heartfelt. My apology to Tiffany that her beautiful full-color maps needed to be printed in black and whilte. The colored maps are worthy of framing and display.

Five individuals further verified this story and all gave credence to various portions: Marion Zubrzycki, Risa Fragale, Eli Pollinger, Barbara Wolfrum, and Robert (Bob) Young. It is with a very heavy heart that during the writing of this book, Uncle Marion (age 92) and dear friend Risa (age 95) passed on, both of who shared in Dad's life story. Yet, happily, as the circle of life goes on, also during the writing of this book, Dad's great grandson, Wesley John Zale, was born.

A heartfelt appreciation goes out to all my family members: Zales, Antoniks, and Zubrzyckis. They were the cheerleaders, were supportive, and offered encouragement.

Thank you to very special people in my life: Nancy Burzynski, Karen Jans-Orlando, and Kerry Skochin. They read various chapters, listened to my moaning and groaning while trying to put words to paper, offered critiques, and unending support. It was years ago that prisoner of war stories were shared with Dorothy Johler Bryan and Pat and Au Wang. Dorothy's father, Jacob "Jake" Johler, was with Dad in Mukden. Pat and Au gave unselfishly of their time and finances to the preservation of what remains today of the POW camp at Mukden, now called Shenyang, China.

It was an honor to be granted permission to quote from James Bollich's book, "A Soldier's Journal." Mr. Bollich and Dad were both interned at Mukden. He gave a copy of his book to Dad with the inscription, "To John Zale – An Ex-POW who went through the same experiences as I did. This book should bring back memories of those times. Times that were not pleasant, and memories that cannot, and should not, be forgotten. – James J. Bollich 7/22/94."

Photo credits in Chapter 4 go to the American Ex-Prisoners of War, National Headquarters, Arlington, Texas. Dad was a member of this organization, and now, I too, am a member.

Ron Krul, Military of the Purple Heart, how can I thank you enough for all your support for the special dedication held at the Boy Scout camp for Dad and for this book. You were his friend, and you live a life of self-sacrifice for fellow patriots, just as Dad did.

How can this list be complete without mentioning Dad's Boy Scout Troop 192. Thank you to Paul Sikora, Richard Kloch, Raymond Budnik, and all of Dad's scouts. You all gave him a purpose in life. He could not have dealt with the nightmares of being a POW without the time, love, and energy he poured into "his Scouts."

Personally, I cannot even express my deepest and most sincere thanks to those men and women who have served, and are serving, in our military. Without their sacrifices, I would not be enjoying all the wonderful freedoms today that we take for granted. "Thank you for your Service" doesn't come close to my indebtedness to you.

To God be the Glory for inspiring me to be a voice for the voiceless. "And not only that, but we also glory in tribulations, knowing that tribulation produces perseverance; and perseverance, character; and character, hope." Romans 5:3-4, NKJV.

REFERENCES

"The Will to Survive" is a biographical account of John Zale's life. Anecdotal evidence in describing his personal experience was relied upon and in the context of historical incidents. Personal testimonies, represented by typical experiences of other prisoners of war, were verified through stories obtained from the sources listed below:

"A Soldier's Journal," by James Bollich

"Kill All Order" from the National Archives, Washington, DC

"The Japanese Story," American Ex-POW, Inc., National Medical Research Comm.

"Death March—The Survivors of Bataan," by Donald Knox

"The Story of World War II," by Robert Leckie (Random House) Copyright 1964

Mukden photos: Source unknown, possibly by Joe Vater

American Ex-Prisoners of War, National Headquarters, Arlington, Texas

"Polar Bear Regiment" from Camp Drum website

Wikipedia –information belonging to the public domain and is not subject to copyright

Wikimedia –image of Carabao patch of the 31st Infantry Regiment

Every effort was made to locate individuals mentioned in this book in order to obtain permissions to use their names. Any omission is regretted and unintentional.

Appendix A

Polar Bear Insignia
The 31st Infantry Regiment

"Pro Patria" means "For Country." The 31st Infantry Regiment (Polar Bears) is known as the "American Foreign Legion" because this unit has never been stationed in the United States since its formation on August 13, 1916.

The United States Army Forces Far East (USAFFE) was made up of both Filipino and American troops. John Zale related that there were two shoulder patches worn as part of the "Philippine Division" of the 31st Infantry. Both patches were authorized in 1922.

The "Philippine Division" patch was created based on two US infantry regiments (15th and 31st) and two Philippine Scout regiments. One was the "Carabao" patch, which featured a gold carabao, symbolizing the Philippines, on a red background. The other patch was the "Sea Lion," representing a white sea lion, taken from the historical coat of arms of the City of Manila.

General Douglas MacArthur stated, "There is no unit in the American Army which has served with greater distinction, both in peace and in war, than has the 31st Infantry. As the advance element in our Pacific defense, the regiment has always performed its assigned mission with marked gallantry and commendable precision. At Bataan it achieved its greatest glory as its lines held firm time and again against the assaults of overwhelming superior force. It now faces a future of continued service in our country's honor, duty, and sacrifice which will be an inspiration for American Armies for all time to come."

During the Battle of Bataan, MacArthur ordered 5,000 men, including the 31st, to fight a delaying action against elements of the Japanese. The 31st incurred heavy casualties by the time it rejoined the main defensive line at Abucay on January 9, 1942. Despite dwindling supplies and mounting losses, the 31st and other units defending Bataan managed to halt the Japanese advance and forced them to withdraw and await reinforcements over the next several weeks before renewing their offensive. It was here, on the Abucay line, that Corporal John Zubrzycki was wounded in action on January 21, 1942.

Appendix B

Don't EVER give up!

Appendix C

"The Light of Integrity"

*The soul is dyed the color of its thoughts.
Think only on those things that are in
line with your principles and can bear
the full light of day.
The content of your character is your
choice. Day by day, what you choose,
what you think, and what you do is who
you become.
Your integrity is your destiny....it is the
light that guides your way.*

Heraclitus
Greek poet, philosopher

Soli Deo Gloria

To the Glory of God Alone